Reforming Trade Policy
in Papua New Guinea and the Pacific Islands

Reprints Collection:
Economics

As well as being established to publish high quality refereed new works the University of Adelaide Press selects previously published books by staff for reprinting both electronically and as soft-cover books.

Strengthening the Global Trading System

Indonesia in a Reforming World Economy

Reforming Trade Policy in Papua New Guinea and the Pacific Islands

The Economics of Quarantine

Global Wine Markets, 1961-2003

The Building of Economics at Adelaide
(Barr Smith Press imprint)

Reforming Trade Policy
in Papua New Guinea and the Pacific Islands

Kym Anderson and Michael Bosworth

UNIVERSITY OF
ADELAIDE PRESS

THE UNIVERSITY
OF ADELAIDE
AUSTRALIA

SUB CRUCE LUMEN

Published in Adelaide by

The University of Adelaide Press
Level 1, 254 North Terrace
University of Adelaide
South Australia
5005
press@adelaide.edu.au
www.adelaide.edu.au/press

The University of Adelaide Press publishes externally refereed scholarly books by staff of the University of Adelaide. It aims to maximise the accessibility to its best research by publishing works through the internet as free downloads and as high quality printed volumes on demand.

Electronic Index: this book is available as a downloadable PDF with fully searchable text.

This book is a facsimile republication. Some minor errors may remain. Originally published by the Centre for International Economic Studies, University of Adelaide, and the Institute of National Affairs, Port Moresby.

First published 2000
Republished 2009

Subject Keywords:
World Trade Organisation - Asia Pacific Economic Cooperation – Papua New Guinea Commercial Policy – Papua New Guinea Foreign Economic Relations – Oceania Commercial Policy – Oceania Foreign Economic Relations

For the full **Cataloguing-in-Publication** data please contact National Library of Australia: cip@nla.gov.au

ISBN 978-0-9806238-2-6 (electronic)
ISBN 978-0-9806238-9-5 (paperback)

Cover image: iStockphoto
Cover design: Chris Tonkin

Contents

List of charts, tables and boxes

Foreword

It is almost impossible for a meeting to be held in the world to discuss international economic issues without it being disrupted by violent demonstrations. Papua New Guineans are not immune to the distrust and bewilderment that surround these issues which affect all of us. As is so often the case when we don't understand something we hit out blindly at it. The World Bank, the IMF, WTO and APEC are all institutions that come under this mantle. They are blamed for almost everything that is supposed to be wrong with our lives.

It is fashionable to blame these institutions and the easy part is that those who do blame them can do so by merely calling their names rather than having to justify their stands or provide any evidence for what they are saying. This study is aimed at providing a reasoned argument about the effects of WTO and APEC, primarily how they affect PNG but also about how they affect other small Pacific nations.

PNG is a trading nation and will be one for a long time to come. We rely on exports for our income and our growth and we need to create the best possible conditions in which our exporters can sell to the rest of the world. There is nothing wrong with being a trading nation and many of the world's richest nations got there because they were good traders. PNG needs to stimulate all of its exports and to create conditions that will encourage new ones. It cannot afford to retain barriers that make the cost of exports higher.

The INA has long been concerned about this subject. Its concern has been whether PNG will be able to carry out the necessary adjustments and how it will be able to absorb business and workers who are replaced by the changes. This worry comes because of the smallness and disparity of the PNG economy and the lack of obvious alternative investments to absorb the displaced capital and labour.

There are many reasons why there has not been enough investment in PNG and tariff protection has only been one of them. It has embraced the WTO and APEC agenda enthusiastically, some would say too quickly and too willingly. This study makes the very important point that the expected improvements for a more liberal trade policy will only work if the rest of the economy is freed up and resources are encouraged into new ventures because investors see that there are markets available and profits to be made.

The best wage, price and employment policies will only emerge as a result of good and liberal economic policies. Governments are not good at setting wages or prices because they don't have the pressures of competition and they tend to reflect the prejudices of a small group of people. Protection looks after small interest groups and has tended to encourage corruption as those interest groups try to protect their privileged positions. Competition, or even the threat of competition, forces firms and traders to seek the cheapest methods of production and makes them pass on these benefits to the rest of the economy.

The study has paid particular attention to PNG's sugar industry because it is a classic example of the problems that a small economy faces when it encourages, through protection from import competition and other measures, a large investment in a remote area. There are around 10,000 people in some way dependant on Ramu for their livelihood, either as employees, outgrowers, suppliers or their families. Ramu has provided infrastructure to a remote area and it will be hard to replace. Nevertheless, the authors believe that PNG would be better off keeping to the proposed reduction on tariffs even if that forced the closure of Ramu. They argue that the substantial adjustment costs to those 10,000 people would not outweigh the benefits that the rest of the population will gain (a) directly from cheaper sugar prices for food processors and final consumers and, more importantly, (b) indirectly from the faster growth in the rest of the economy that the reforms will stimulate. The authors acknowledge that in extreme cases such as Ramu the government may need to design temporary adjustment assistance schemes. Costly and unfair though such schemes are (because if adjusters in other industries/regions were to be compensated there would be a budget blowout), sometimes they are necessary politically when the alternative would be to exempt such groups from reform.

Initially we tried to find someone from the Pacific or South East Asia to do the study. For a variety of reasons we were unsuccessful. We then approached Professor Kym Anderson from Adelaide University who agreed to take on the assignment with Malcolm Bosworth. Both are strong supporters of the multilateral trading system, having each spend several years working at the GATT/WTO Secretariat. They see the gains from trade as far outweighing the short term costs that will be felt as adjustments are made to allow greater gains from trade to flow. This paper sets out their reasoning for this stance.

The INA is grateful to AusAID and Ramu Sugar Ltd for the sponsorship of this study. Ramu has been given the opportunity to comment on the first draft of the study and the authors have taken these into account when finalising the report. We also thank Kym Anderson and Malcolm Bosworth for their contributions as well as all those people who gave their time to be interviewed and who attended the public seminar on the subject.

Michael Manning, Director
Institute of National Affairs

Preface

The terms of reference of this study, which was commissioned by PNG's Institute of National Affairs, require it to:

- identify the costs and benefits to PNG of compliance with WTO and APEC;
- identify industries that may be affected and profile them in terms of employment, original capital investment, (if possible) written down capital values, government commitments including equity, protection, tax incentives;
- make suggestions about how PNG can best adjust/adapt to compliance with WTO and APEC conditions;
- identify short and long term measures that PNG and other (larger) member states can take to minimize the short-term costs of compliance (which should look at removing structural rigidities over a planned time scale, interventions that might make PNG industry more competitive such as additional research funding, identification of alternative investment opportunities and possible structural adjustment assistance measures);
- identify any other measures that PNG should be taking to improve its competitive position in both the short and long term; and
- identify any other likely problems from compliance with WTO and APEC.

The report was prepared following a one-week visit to PNG by Malcolm Bosworth, from 6 June 2000. Discussions were held with PNG officials from relevant ministries as well as representatives of key business groups and industries (Appendix 1). A public seminar on 'WTO and APEC' was organized by the Institute of National Affairs and held in Port Moresby on 9 June 2000 (Appendix 2). The seminar raised several important issues relating to PNG's WTO and APEC involvement. The presentations outlined the Government's views, including the Investment Promotion Authority, as well as those of manufacturers and non-government organizations. The seminar provided a useful dialogue with the audience on PNG's membership of the WTO and APEC. It demonstrated that there was general support from policymakers and industry representatives for PNG to actively participate in the WTO and APEC. However, there was also widespread community anxiety and concerns about the possible adverse impact that globalization and other WTO/APEC initiatives may have on PNG and regional island economies.

About the Authors

Malcolm Bosworth is Senior Research Fellow in the Australia-Japan Research Centre of the Asia Pacific School of Economics and Management, at the Australian National University. He was for many years a government economist advising on Australian trade and industry policies. From 1989-95 he worked at the GATT (now WTO) Secretariat completing Trade Policy Reviews of member countries. His specialty is trade policy and he has been a consultant to numerous international institutions, including the WTO. He has authored and co-authored several publications on the South Pacific.

Kym Anderson is Professor of Economics and Foundation Director of the Centre for International Economic Studies at the University of Adelaide and a Fellow of the Academy of Social Sciences in Australia. During 1990-92 he worked as deputy to the director of economic research at the GATT (now WTO) Secretariat in Geneva, and since 1996 he has served on a series of dispute settlement panels at the World Trade Organization. He also served on the panel advising the Ministers for Foreign Affairs and Trade in their preparation of Australia's first White Paper on Foreign and Trade Policy (1996-97). He has also been a consultant to numerous national and international bureaucracies, business organisations and corporations. His research interests and publications are in the areas of international trade and development, and agricultural and resource economics. He has published 14 books in the trade policy/WTO area as well as more than 150 journal articles and chapters in other books. In 1989 Asia Pacific Press published his *Growth, Structural Change and Economic Policy in Papua New Guinea* (with F.G. Jarrett).

Acronyms

ACP	Africa, Caribbean and Pacific Members of the Lome Convention
ADB	Asian Development Bank
AFTA	ASEAN Free Trade Area
AMS	Aggregate Measure of Support
ANZCERTA	Australia New Zealand Closer Economic Relations Trade Agreement
APEC	Asia Pacific Economic Cooperation
ASEAN	Association of South East Asian Nations
ASYCUDA	Automatic System for Customs Data
ATC	Agreement on Textiles and Clothing
CAP	Common Agricultural Policies
CMIC	Consultative Implementation and Monitoring Council of PNG
DSB	Dispute Settlement Body
ESCAP	Economic and Social Commission for Asia and the Pacific
EVSL	Early Voluntary Sectoral Liberalization
EU	European Union
FIAS	Foreign Investment Advisory Service
FICs	Forum Island Countries
FTA	Free Trade Area
GATT	General Agreement on Tariffs and Trade
GSP	Generalized System of Preferences
IAB	Industries Assistance Board of PNG
IAP	Individual Action Plan (of an APEC member's reform program)
IMF	International Monetary Fund
ISO	International Standards Organization
ITC	International Trade Centre
LDCs	Least-Developed Countries
MFA	Multilateral Fibre Arrangement

MFN	Most Favoured Nation
MSG	Melanesian Spearhead Group
MTN	Multilateral Trade Negotiations
NAQIA	National Agriculture Quarantine Inspection Authority of PNG
OECD	Organisation for Economic Cooperation and Development
PATCRA	Papua New Guinea-Australia Trade and Commercial Relations Agreement
PECC	Pacific Economic Cooperation Committee
PNG	Papua New Guinea
S&D	Special and differential (treatment of developing countries in WTO)
SME	Small and Medium (non-farm) Enterprise
SOE	State-Owned Enterprise
SPARTECA	South Pacific Regional Trade and Economic Cooperation Agreement
SPS	Sanitary and Phytosanitary (Agreement)
STE	State Trading Enterprises
TRIMs	Trade-Related Investment Measures (Agreement)
TRIPs	Trade-Related Intellectual Property (Agreement)
TPRM	Trade Policy Review Mechanism
TRQ	Tariff-Rate Quotas
UNCTAD	United Nations Conference on Trade and Development
UNDP	United Nations Development Programme
USA	United States of America
USITC	United States International Trade Commission
VAT	Value-Added Tax
VER	'Voluntary' Export Restraint
WCO	World Customs Organization
WIPO	World Intellectual Property Organization
WTO	World Trade Organization

Executive summary

Major market reforms needed to raise regional economic growth ...

The countries of the South Pacific have struggled to generate sustainable economic growth since their independence. Interventionist policies have failed in the past here, as they have in all other regions. Business and government leaders in this region are now beginning to acknowledge — as has happened in many other developing country regions over the past two decades — that major reforms are needed to put their economies onto a higher growth path.

... building on tentative beginnings

In most other regions many developing countries have already abandoned those inward-looking policy regimes in preference to growth-enhancing, market-friendly policies. In PNG and the South Pacific, by contrast, only a tentative beginning is evident.

Delaying policy reforms becoming more costly ...

Yet delaying the implementation of trade and investment policy reforms is becoming ever-more costly. This is because in the past decade or so the world has changed in very fundamental ways. The changes affect all economies, but especially those with policy regimes least suited to this fundamentally new environment.

... because globalization with its many benefits is here to stay due to the information revolution

The birth of APEC in 1989, and more so the coming into being of the World Trade Organization in 1995 following the Uruguay Round, have contributed to the new global environment. But they are less a cause of those fundamental changes than a response to them. It is the information technology revolution that is the main driver of the new wave of globalization.

Open economies are best placed to benefit from globalization...

The abilities of national economies to adjust and take advantage of the opportunities offered by globalization differ greatly, but not so much because of different levels of economic development. Rather, it is correlated with differences in the degree of openness of their economies, together with having appropriate institutions for good governance.

... and more so in the future than in the past

A positive feature of globalization is that countries with good economic governance will be rewarded more in the future than they would have been in the past for their sensible policy stance. But the converse is also true. That is, countries with poor economic governance will be penalized more in the future than they would have been in the past. The most obvious manifestation of the penalty for poor governance is the way in which foreign investment is withdrawn and/or stays away. A less obvious but probably more important manifestation is a reduced ability of domestic firms to compete internationally.

WTO and APEC assist national governments respond to globalization

The WTO agreements and the APEC process are crucial international institutional creations aimed at helping national governments respond to the forces of globalization. Key members are responding, and as a consequence globalization has accelerated — making it all the more imperative for other countries to adjust their policy regimes.

The choice is stark

Thus Pacific countries face a stark choice: either they embrace globalization by adjusting their policy regimes to this brave new world, or their economies are destined to grow slower. And they will grow slower not only relative to the rest of the world, but also in absolute terms as they fall further behind the technology leaders.

WTO can help ...

For PNG, Fiji and the Solomon Islands, their WTO membership has the potential to assist their governments adjust their policy regimes in appropriate way. So too does the WTO accession process for those less-populous island economies that have already applied (Samoa, Tonga and Vanuatu). And by becoming a WTO Observer, the South Pacific Forum Secretariat could assist the other Pacific island economies in learning the basic rules of good economic governance as they relate to trade, in essence what GATT/WTO disciplines are about.

... as can APEC

The APEC process provides a supplementary avenue for learning about good economic governance. As an APEC member, PNG can acquire that directly; but FICs can get it indirectly through their close association not only with PNG but also with their other neighbours who are members.

Successfully meeting the reform challenge will produce larger pay-offs ...

A crucial challenge for Pacific island governments and their citizens is thus before them. On the one hand, if they choose not to open up and reform their economies, their relatively poor economic growth and poverty alleviation performance of the past 25 years is likely not just to continue but to worsen. On the other hand, if they choose to embrace reform, the payoff will be even higher now than it would have been without this new wave of globalization. This is because Pacific island economies are further behind than they were even just a few years ago, and because the opportunities for leapfrogging via technology transfer are so much greater now thanks to the information revolution.

... but political and social resistance to reforms must be overcome

Like anything worthwhile in life, embracing that challenge will not be easy politically or socially. Vested interests in the current protectionist trade regimes will fight to retain their privileged positions. Others will resent having to adjust to new ways of doing things. Hence politicians with a short horizon will be reluctant to risk their positions by taking the lead, and may themselves have a vested bias in resisting change. Yet the 'status quo' option will become increasingly costly as globalization proceeds in the rest of the world. So how can Pacific island economies begin to respond?

Pacific island governments must build a constituency for reform ...

The most important priority for governments is to accept — and persuade their constituencies to accept — that trade, investment and other economic reforms are badly needed if private sector development and growth is to occur, since it is only by improving productivity that living standards can rise over the long term. Governments must be deeply committed to the process, and because that commitment has to be sustained it must be driven from a domestic base. While WTO (and APEC) membership can help reform-minded governments to implement market-opening measures, membership alone is insufficient for meaningful and sustainable reform.

... by raising awareness of the opportunities, but also the adjustment costs

First, communities need to become much more acutely aware of the gains that could come their way if WTO-consistent market reforms were adopted. They also need to be aware that the gains would come gradually rather than all at once, whereas the costs of adjustment as reforms are implemented — even though they are one-off — will have to be borne up front. In the case of grossly distorted economies, the adjustment period could stretch out over a decade or more. If that is not understood at the outset, the risk is that disappointed expectations could lead to pressures for policy reversals — which could be worse than doing nothing, because it would involve double adjustment costs and no gains. But the prospect of a prolonged and difficult adjustment period is no reason to abandon the reforms. Rather, it is an incentive to commence now before the costs escalate even further.

Prioritize and sequence reforms and phase-in the bigger changes

Second, reforms need to be prioritized so they are appropriately sequenced and implemented at a pace that does not overwhelm the capacity of the legislature and the public administrators. A key to keeping the costs of adjustment manageable is to phase in the bigger reform programs over a pre-determined period that is announced at the outset. Thinking through the new policies before announcing them is crucial though, since subsequent changes to the new policies — or even just to the timing of the implementation phases — will reduce the credibility of the process and thereby discourage investors.

Education and training are the best means of facilitating adjustment

Third, even though the benefits from market liberalization will far outweigh the up-front adjustment costs, the latter are both immediate and hit concentrated groups. Where such interest groups are powerful politically, reform may only be possible in extreme cases if those affected are given an explicit adjustment incentive. But otherwise the best way the government can facilitate adjustment — which because of economic growth and globalization abroad is going to happen to a considerable extent even when policies are unchanged — is to better equip people with the necessary skills for meeting the challenges and seizing the opportunities that change brings. All the international evidence points to better basic education being the key provider of such skills, so some of the tax dividend from the faster economic growth that will result from reform might be used to improve the quantity and quality of education. As well, training programs for administrators and for trainers of administrators could enhance the capacity of the public service to facilitate adjustment to the reforms.

Seek international help for reform

And fourth, Pacific island economies need not try to respond to these challenges alone. They can support each other by sharing ideas on how to design and implement reforms, and seek technical and economic help from the WTO Secretariat, the World Bank, UNCTAD, the Forum Secretariat and (for PNG at least) though the APEC process, as well as via bilateral aid programs.

A great opportunity is there to be seized

The opportunity to embrace the reform process more comprehensively, and the rewards for doing so, have never been greater than they are now. It remains for leaders of Pacific islands to seize that opportunity.

1

Introduction

Slow growth continues to disappoint

Papua New Guinea (PNG) and other (South) Pacific island economies have struggled to generate sustainable economic growth. Despite continuing to receive very large amounts of donor assistance per capita from bilateral and multilateral agencies, most economies of the region seem to be no closer to achieving this goal than they were a decade or two ago.

Views on accepting the need for economic reforms are changing ...

However, governments and business leaders in the region are beginning to acknowledge that major reforms are needed to put their economies on a sustainable growth path. Fundamental market-opening and other economic reforms are essential, along with strengthening of their institutional settings and governance. Leaders now recognize that past interventionist policies have failed in this region as they have elsewhere, and that many other developing countries have abandoned them in the past decade or so in preference to growth-enhancing market-friendly policies.

... and action plans are being endorsed

For example, Forum Island Countries (FICs) adopted a plan of action in 1995 to promote their economic development beyond 2000. This consisted of reforms to 13 sets of policies of the sort widely accepted from international experience as necessary for establishing an economic environment for sustained growth. It includes reduced trade barriers, tax reform, civil service reform, and corporatization and privatization of public utilities. The plan was endorsed at subsequent meetings of the South Pacific Forum Leaders' and Economic Ministers' meetings.

There have been regional trade initiatives such as SPARTECA, Lome and PATCRA ...

In seeking to reform trade policies, the region has embraced some international trade agreements in the past. For example, there is a long history of regional trading arrangements involving Pacific island economies that provide them with non-reciprocated preferential access to developed-country markets. Exports from PNG, Fiji, Samoa, Solomon Islands, Tonga, Tuvalu and Vanuatu have entered the European Union (EU) free of import duties and quantitative restrictions under the Lome Convention since 1978. Such arrangements are being extended for a further transitional period of eight years from March 2000 under a Partnership Agreement with the ACP (Asia, Caribbean and Pacific) countries following expiration of Lome IV, after which a reciprocal free trade agreement is mooted[1]. Australia and New Zealand have provided similar access to exports from FICs since 1981 under the South Pacific Regional Trade and Economic Cooperation Agreement (SPARTECA). PNG has also had a bilateral agreement with Australia since independence that establishes a non-reciprocal free trade area whereby its exports enter Australia duty free (the PNG Australia Trade and Commercial Relations Agreement, PATCRA). In addition, PNG is considering whether to seek full membership of the Association of South East Asian Nations (ASEAN), in which it is currently an observer, and thereby to AFTA (the ASEAN Free Trade Area).

... and the MSG

As well, members of the Melanesian Spearhead Group (MSG), initially PNG, Solomon Islands and Vanuatu and subsequently New Caledonia and Fiji, provide each other with limited tariff preferences. PNG and Fiji also have had a limited reciprocal trade agreement since 1996.

---

[1] The EU is currently waiting on a decision following its request for a waiver in the WTO for these transitional arrangements.

An FTA also is being proposed

A free-trade area, currently being negotiated among FICs on the basis of negative lists of exempt products to be excluded from the preferential arrangements, is planned for implementation in 2001[2]. Tariffs on goods are to be eliminated over a number of years (yet to be specified). The effects of including services trade and of extending the agreement to French and U.S. Pacific island territories, and of longer term integration with the Closer Economic Relations Trade Agreement between Australia and New Zealand (ANZCERTA), are also being examined.

Some Pacific island economies are also looking beyond the region ...

Despite these regional developments having the primary objective of integrating Pacific island economies into the world economy, their trade and investment patterns remain narrowly based in terms of direction and composition, and somewhat dependant on those preferential trading arrangements, especially for manufactured goods. Meanwhile, globalization is inexorably influencing the region in ways that are rewarding more than in the past those economies that have good economic governance — but also, for reasons discussed in the next chapter, are penalizing more than in the past those economies whose policies are inhibiting efficient resource use.

... to the WTO ...

To break out of the narrowness of current trade relations, some Pacific island economies are increasingly turning their attention outside the region to the World Trade Organization (WTO) to help jump-start and/or consolidate their economic reforms. Three island economies, Fiji, Papua New Guinea and the Solomon Islands, participated in the Uruguay Round and became founding members of the WTO by virtue of their previous status within the GATT[3]. These countries were not therefore required to

---

[2] The FICs are the Cook Islands, Federated States of Micronesia, Fiji, Kiribati, Republic of the Marshall Islands, Nauru, Niue, Palau, Papua New Guinea, Solomon Islands, Tonga, Tuvalu, Vanuatu and Samoa.

[3] Fiji has been a full contracting party to the GATT since November 1993, and became a founding WTO member in January 1996. PNG and the Solomon Islands, de facto GATT members because of their

undertake the lengthy and at times arduous accession process that any aspiring new WTO member must now undergo – a process in which three other island economies are currently engaged. Vanuatu and Tonga formally applied for WTO membership in 1995, and Samoa in 1998. Vanuatu's accession is the most advanced, but is still some way from being completed. An initial draft of the Working Party Report has been circulated to members, and consultations on terms and conditions of accession are continuing. Tonga circulated to WTO members its Memorandum on the Foreign Trade Regime in May 1998. The South Pacific Forum Secretariat has also obtained observer status to the WTO on certain committees, such as the Committee on Trade and Development, and has played an important advisory role in support of those Pacific countries' accession.

... and APEC

A further opportunity to consolidate and strengthen unilateral reform is provided through the Asia Pacific Economic Cooperation (APEC) process. PNG joined APEC in 1994 and is the only Pacific island member. Although seen as a regional arrangement, its diverse membership in the Asia Pacific region covers 21 countries[4]. Most APEC economies also belong to the WTO[5]. All APEC economies are committed to the 1994 Bogor objectives of voluntarily achieving 'free and open trade and investment' in developed economies by 2010, and in all developing member countries by 2020. PNG is therefore committed to comprehensive liberalization, including of agriculture and

---

past protectorate status with Australia and the Unites Kingdom, respectively, exercised their rights during the change-over to become founding WTO members. PNG became a WTO member in June 1996, and the Solomon Islands from December 1996.

[4] APEC economies are Australia, Brunei Darussalam, Canada, Chile, China, Hong Kong China, Indonesia, Japan, Korea, Malaysia, Mexico, New Zealand, PNG, the Philippines, Singapore, Chinese Taipei, Thailand, the US and, since 1999, Peru, the Russian Federation and Vietnam.

[5] Of the 21 APEC economies, 17 are currently WTO members. China and Chinese Taipei are now expected to join the WTO by end-2000 or in 2001. Vietnam and Russia are a little further behind in the process of WTO accession.

services, on a non-discriminatory basis, fully consistent with the WTO. PNG submitted APEC Individual Action Plans (IAPs) for liberalization following the Osaka Action Agenda in 1996, and again in 1998. It also participated in the so-called Early Voluntary Sectoral Liberalization (EVSL) initiative, aimed at advancing trade liberalization in certain sectors. APEC economies transferred these sectoral initiatives to reduce tariffs in these sectors to the WTO, while continuing to advance liberalization of non-tariff measures in these sectors in a concerted unilateral fashion.

Outline of the Study

This study begins in Chapter 2 by examining the growth record of key Pacific island economies and identifying the reasons for their relatively poor performance. It then looks in Chapter 3 at the process of globalization that is affecting those and indeed all economies increasingly; and the role the WTO (assisted by APEC) has played in that process. It also examines their implications for the development strategies of countries seeking to improve their economic performance in this rapidly changing international environment.

Taking the necessary steps to reform and open up an economy is never easy politically for any government. This is because the necessary costs of structural adjustments are immediate and often highly concentrated on a few groups whereas the gains from that adjustment — even though they usually far outweigh the adjustment costs — are diffuse and take time to show themselves. Bearing that in mind, Chapter 4 looks at what policy reforms are needed to revitalize the PNG economy and, by example, other Pacific island nations, including the important roles played by trade and investment liberalization to promote competitive markets and economic restructuring. Chapter 5 shows how the WTO can help to facilitate regional economic development and discusses the sensitive issue of compliance costs of such membership. The supplementary role that APEC can play is outlined in Chapter 6. Chapter 7 concludes by pointing to the policy implications of WTO and APEC membership for PNG and other Pacific island economies and the stark choices facing them.

While the study focuses mainly on PNG, because it is both a WTO and APEC member, its findings are also relevant to the two other island economies that are already in the WTO. It is also particularly timely for the region's prospective WTO members (Vanuatu, Samoa and Tonga) and for others contemplating joining.

2

Performance of Pacific Island Economies

Poor growth record of PNG and other Pacific nations ...

PNG and other Pacific island economies, although varying somewhat between countries and years, have performed relatively poorly for decades (final column of Table 2.1). In real terms per capita GDP has risen less than 1 per cent per year during the past twenty five years except in the Solomon Islands. That compares with around 4 per cent in Southeast Asia and in low-income countries as a group. PNG, the largest economy by far, has been among the worst performers, despite its huge mineral and petroleum wealth. In the 1980s its GDP grew only 1.9 per cent while its population was growing at above 2.2 per cent, meaning per capita GDP fell at 0.3 per cent per year. It recovered in the period 1990 to 1999, growing at 1.7 per cent per capita (World Bank 2000b). The latter growth occurred mainly in the first half of the 1990s though: GNP per head has declined again since the mid-1990s, when it was above US$1,100, to $US800 in 1999[6].

---

[6] GNP is GDP plus foreign earnings by nationals minus domestic earnings by foreigners.

Table 2.1 Key economic indicators for selected Pacific Island and other economies, 1999

	Popul-ation 1999	Population per sq km 1999	Pop'n annual growth rate 1993-98	GNP per head 1999	GNP, total 1999	GNP per head, PPP basis 1999	Real GDP per capita growth 1975-98
	'000		per cent per yr	current US$	current US$ m	US$	% per year
Pacific islands							
Papua New Guinea	4,710	10	2.3	800	3,746	2,260	0.2
Fiji	801	44	1.0	2,210	1,771	4,540	0.6
Kiribati	88	121	na	910	81	3,190	na
W. Samoa	170	60	0.7	1,060	181	3,920	0.3
Solomon Is.	429	15	3.3	750	320	1,950	2.6
Tonga	100	138	0.4	1,720	172	4,280	na
Vanuatu	189	16	2.7	1,170	221	2,770	-0.8
SE Asia							
Indonesia	207,000	114	1.7	580	119,500	2,440	4.1
Malaysia	23,000	69	2.5	3,400	77,300	7,960	3.9
Thailand	62,000	121	1.3	1,960	121,000	5,600	4.9
Caribbean							
Antigua & Barbuda	67	153	0.6	8,300[a]	555[a]	9,440[a]	4.6
Barbados	267	620	0.4	7,890[a]	2,096[a]	12,260[a]	1.6
St Lucia	154	253	1.6	3,770	580	5,020	3.6
Indian Ocean							
Maldives	278	925	2.6	1,160	332	3,550	5.1
Mauritius	1,170	576	1.1	3,590	4,203	8,650	4.3
Seychelles	80	177	1.4	6,540	520	10,380	3.1
ALL LOW-INCOME		73	2.0	410		1,790	3.4
ALL LOWER MIDDLE INCOME		48	1.1	1,200		3,960	3.7

[a] 1998

. *Source:* World Bank (2000a,b) and, for final column, UNDP (2000).

... even compared with other island economies

The growth in per capita GNP of Pacific island economies has been slow even compared with the similar-sized island economies of the Indian Ocean and Caribbean (Table 2.1). All Pacific island economies now rank between 100th and 150th in the listing of the world's 206 economies when ordered by current GNP per capita (as measured using the World Bank *Atlas* method involving a three-year average foreign exchange rate). These data differ from the purchasing power parity per capita GNP data shown in the final column of Table 2.1. The latter usually are much higher for developing countries, but the rankings do not change markedly. In PNG's case, its PPP level was US$2,260 in 1999, and its PPP ranking was 147 out of 206 economies, compared with a ranking of 138 using the current dollar method[7]. So instead of being two-thirds of the lower middle-income country average as with the current dollar measure of GNP, it is just over half that group's average as measured in PPP terms.

Island economies range from least-developed to middle-income countries

All Pacific island economies are classified by the United Nations as developing economies, with the Solomon Islands, Kiribati, Samoa and Tuvalu considered least-developed economies. PNG is classified by the World Bank as a lower middle-income country. Regional income levels vary markedly within PNG. Those in urban centres exceed rural levels of around US$350 per head by about tenfold. Similar disparities in income levels are also found in other Pacific island economies.

Low growth has meant deteriorating social progress

With the possible exception of Fiji, Pacific island economies continually rate badly on the United Nation's Human Development Index. In the latest rankings, PNG ranked 133rd out of 174 countries (and 129th in 1999), Solomon Islands 121st (118th in 1999), and Vanuatu 118th (116th in 1999). This index is a composite measure of life expectancy, educational levels and PPP-adjusted income. Clearly, PNG's limited growth − mainly from mining − has not been transformed into social progress. While social

---

[7] Purchasing Power Parity (PPP) income is the level in US dollars that would equate real domestic purchasing power or living standards across countries at existing exchange rates.

indicators improved in the first dozen or so years following its independence in 1975, they have deteriorated badly in the past decade. Many of PNG's social indicators are now below the average for low-income countries, including life expectancy, adult literacy and education (Table 2.2).

Main characteristics of Pacific island economies

Some are resource rich

While PNG and other Pacific economies differ in many respects, such as cultural and ethnic backgrounds, they share similar key economic characteristics as small island economies with slow and erratic economic growth that falls well short of potential. Being relatively lightly populated, the larger Pacific island countries are generally rich in natural resources per capita. For example, Fiji, Samoa and the Solomon Islands all have substantial timber and fish resources. PNG is especially fortunate in also having considerable oil and mineral wealth. Even the more densely populated Pacific countries are still much better endowed with land per capita than many in the Caribbean and Indian Ocean (column 2 of Table 2.1).

Economic smallness is a fact of life

Some of these characteristics, such as geographic isolation and physical smallness, cannot be changed. Arguably, however, these are not the only or even the main reasons for bad economic performance in the Pacific. Others are policy-induced features over which governments have control. Understanding the negative effects of these policy measures is central to any assessment of the potential impact that the WTO and APEC may have on PNG and other island economies.

Table 2.2 Key social indicators for selected Pacific Island and other
economies, 1998

	Life expect-ancy	Adult literacy	Education, all levels (average)	Human Dev't Index (HDI)
	years	% > 14 years	% enrolment	rank (out of 174)
Pacific islands				
Papua New Guinea	58	63	37	133
Fiji	73	92	81	66
W. Samoa	72	80	65	95
Solomon Islands	72	62	46	121
Vanuatu	68	64	47	118
South-East Asia				
Indonesia	66	86	65	109
Malaysia	72	86	65	61
Thailand	69	95	61	76
Caribbean				
Antigua & Barbuda	76	95	78	37
Barbados	77	97	80	30
St Lucia	70	82	68	88
Indian Ocean				
Maldives	65	96	75	89
Mauritius	72	84	63	71
Seychelles	71	84	76	53
ALL LOW-INCOME COUNTRIES	**63**	**69**	**56**	
ALL MEDIUM-INCOME COUNTRIES	**69**	**88**	**73**	

. Source: UNDP (2000).

Vulnerability of small economies to external shocks

PNG is by far the largest island economy

Pacific island economies are small by world and regional standards. For example, the combined GDP of the ten largest Pacific island economies in 1999 amounted to barely $US7 billion, compared to $US53 billion for New Zealand. There is considerable difference in the size of Pacific island economies, with the GDP of PNG being more than twice that of the next largest and much more affluent economy of Fiji.

The region is vulnerable to external shocks ...

Due to their smallness, such economies are narrowly based and somewhat vulnerable to periodic economic shocks induced by adverse international conditions, such as sharp declines in their terms of trade. For example, the recent rise in the world price of petroleum has impacted heavily on these economies which are reliant on imports of petroleum products[8]. Similarly, the Solomon Islands and PNG were adversely affected by the decline in world log prices following the Asian economic crisis, and by depressed mineral prices, especially for gold and copper. Minor changes in the terms of trade can thus translate to major changes in external balances and in economic growth.

... and adverse geographical and climatic factors ...

Economic variability is also increased by geographical and climatic factors. For example, cyclones commonly hit the islands, damaging rural holdings and infrastructure, and droughts occur frequently. PNG, for example, suffered widespread cyclone-related damage to its copra and cocoa crops in 1997. This was followed by a severe drought that not only affected its food crops but also disrupted its major mining operations, including copper production at Ok Tedi due to the Fly River becoming too shallow to transport mine output.

---

[8] In the case of PNG, there is some offset from rising petroleum prices because it also exports crude oil.

... not to mention political instability

The political disruptions in Fiji and the Solomon Islands have added to the economic woes of these countries in the past year or so, just as they did for Fiji following its coup in the late 1980s. Foreign investors (and even nationals) simply park their investable funds elsewhere when such events occur, and typically take a long time to bring them back. This withdrawal of funds raises domestic real interest rates, which are currently above 10% in PNG, and slows capital formation.

Heavy dependence on a large informal agriculture sector

Island economies will continue their reliance on primary production

These islands remain essentially agrarian economies supplemented by some development of other primary resources such as timber, fish and, in the case of especially PNG, oil and mineral (most notably copper and gold) extraction. At the heart of their agriculture is a large informal sector on which economic development for the vast majority of their population depends in a critical way. Policies by individual governments to develop a manufacturing basis have generally achieved little success and in all the Pacific island economies the industrial sector still contributes well under 10 per cent of GDP and employment. This is to be expected given their abundance of natural resources relative to produced capital in the region (see Appendix 4). The services sector, however, is capable of expanding in relative importance, including in wholesaling, retailing, tourism and construction.

The informal sector accounts for much agricultural output ...

The dependence of these economies on the informal agricultural sector is demonstrated by the PNG situation even though, unlike neighbouring islands, it also has a significant mining sector. Primary production in total accounted for 51% of GDP in 1997, agriculture, forestry, and fisheries accounted for nearly two-thirds of that share (Chart 2.1). However, these figures substantially understate the contribution of agriculture when the informal sector is properly taken into account. Commercial agriculture in PNG is supplemented by significant subsistence or semi-commercial food production, estimated to be about half of

Chart 2.1
Sectoral composition of GDP, 1988 and 1997 (at 1983 prices)

Per cent

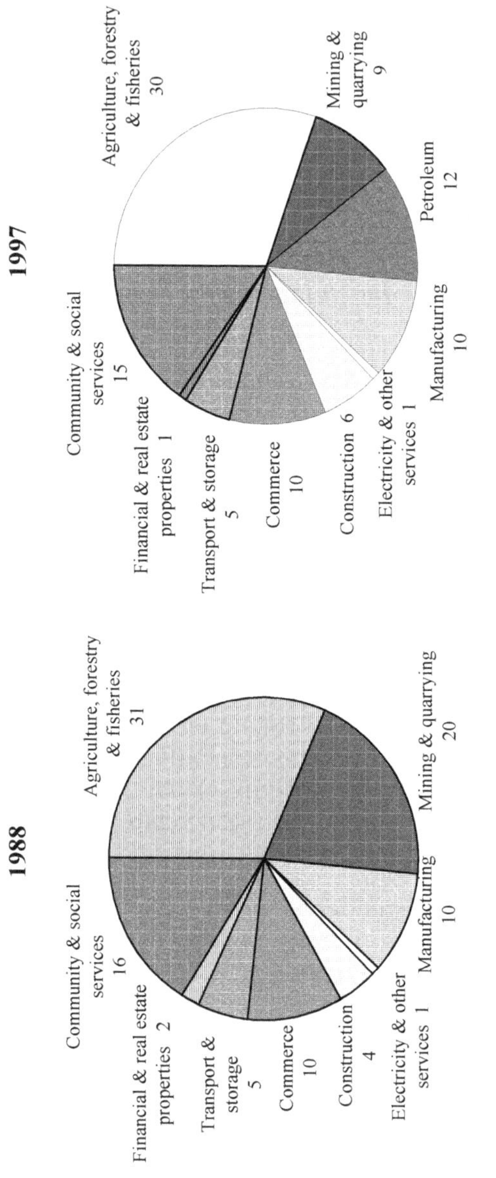

1988

Agriculture, forestry & fisheries
31

Mining & quarrying
20

Manufacturing
10

Construction
4

Commerce
10

Electricity & other services 1

Transport & storage
5

Financial & real estate properties 2

Community & social services
16

Total: US$2.974 billion

1997

Agriculture, forestry & fisheries
30

Mining & quarrying
9

Petroleum
12

Manufacturing
10

Electricity & other services 1

Construction 6

Commerce
10

Transport & storage
5

Financial & real estate properties 1

Community & social services
15

Total: US$4.821 billion

Source: **Papua New Guinea Government,** *Budget Papers* **Vol. 1; and** *Economic and Development Policies*, **various issues.**

total agricultural output. Some 85% of the PNG people live in rural areas and are highly dependant on agriculture, with food gardens largely meeting subsistence needs while cash crops for both export and domestic markets provide cash income. It is estimated that the informal sector produces almost all food in PNG: over 70% of coffee; 65% of cocoa and copra; and 35% of palm oil. Expanding the informal provision of basic services in rural areas is also important to the economy's growth[9].

... and most of employment   Although the primary sector accounts for only around a quarter of formal employment, making it second in importance to the services sector, the significance of agriculture is increased substantially if the informal sector is taken into account. The informal agricultural sector is thought to account for well over two-thirds of the total PNG workforce.

High trade dependency

The external sector of PNG and other neighbouring Pacific islands is relatively large since these economies depend heavily on trade. Not surprisingly, such economies generally have very high trade penetration ratios. Most raw materials and consumer products are imported. Similarly, because of their small markets most of their primary commercial production is exported for further processing. For example, both PNG's imports and exports of goods and services represented around two-thirds of GDP in 1999. This dependence has increased during the past decade, since in 1990 the corresponding shares of GDP were barely two-fifths (World Bank 2000b). Such high trade-to-GDP ratios are to be expected of very small

---

[9] This segment of the economy is not as well developed as in other comparable countries where basic produce markets and the provision of essential repair and other retail services exist on a larger scale. Not least of the reasons for that is the terrain, which ensures the cost of providing transport and communications infrastructure is very high per capita.   There are also regulations restricting the informal provision of services in urban areas.

developing economies. They do not imply that these economies maintain no trade restrictions — indeed most in fact do. But they do underscore the relative importance of trade to their development. Economic growth for these economies is therefore even more closely linked to the strength of the traded sector than is the case for developing countries generally.

Exports (and production) are narrowly based ...

Trade (and production) patterns of Pacific island economies remain narrowly based. Although the precise dependence varies across island nations depending largely on the availability of other natural resources, such as fishing, timber and minerals, these economies remain heavily dependent on agriculture for development. Exports reflect their narrow production base and are concentrated in a few commodities and markets.

... in commodities

Although PNG's oil and minerals account for nearly two-thirds of the total value of exports, agricultural exports, especially of coffee and palm oil, contribute about one-quarter of exports currently. This share has increased substantially from one-sixth in the mid-1990s. In value terms, agricultural exports have more than doubled since then, aided by increased export returns following the currency float and the substantial kina devaluation. Palm oil exports have grown rapidly in recent years, and have replaced the traditional tree crops of cocoa and copra as the second largest agricultural export after coffee (Table 2.3). PNG's palm oil industry appears to offer considerable potential, with its yields already comparing favourably with those of other developing countries.

PNG exports, like other island economies, remain heavily concentrated in a few commodities. In 1998, three commodities, gold, oil and coffee, represented 70% of exports. In the Solomon Islands, the top three exports, forestry, fishing and oil palm, accounted for about 90% of total exports.

Only limited diversification, such as tourism in Fiji

The only economy that has diversified to a limited extent away from the primary sector is Fiji[10]. Nevertheless, its exports are still rather narrowly based — its top three merchandise exports of sugar (38%), garments (22%) and gold (10%) account for more than two-thirds of total merchandise exports. Export diversification is, however, increased by its exporting of tourism services that are equivalent to about one-quarter of merchandise exports. However, while product diversification is to be welcomed, government efforts to encourage such diversity more often then not end up penalizing the traditional industries that are internationally competitive and hence on which economic development still depends heavily.

Heavy dependence on preferential access

Export markets of Pacific island nations remain concentrated geographically. Significant exports are sold to preferential markets, especially the EU, where preferential duty-free access exists under the Lome Convention. Some key exports depend almost exclusively on such markets. For example, over three-quarters of Fiji sugar exports, representing about one-quarter of total merchandise exports, are sold to the UK, at up to double the world price. Similarly, Fiji garment exports are primarily sold to Australia and New Zealand duty-free under SPARTECA, and to the United States under bilateral quotas. Likewise, exports of canned tuna from the region, especially the Solomon Islands, are almost exclusively going to the UK. PNG also exports heavily to Australia under PATCRA and to the EU (including canned tuna) under Lome preferential access. Most exports to other developed markets, such as Japan and the United States, also receive preferential entry under GSP arrangements.

---

[10] However, recent political developments in Fiji culminating in the forced removal of the elected government has been a serious setback for the tourist industry and the economy generally.

Table 2.3 Shares of key commodities in the value of PNG's merchandise exports, 1963 to 1997 (per cent)

	Coconut products	Coffee	Cocoa	Palm Oil	Copper and gold	Forest products	Petroleum	Other	TOTAL
1958-62	48	5	9	0	0	9	0	29	100
1968-72	24	18	11	0	4	7	0	36	100
1983-86	6	15	7	5	40	8	0	19	100
1996-98	3	10	2	6	37	11	27	4	100

Sources: Jarrett and Anderson (1989), updated from AusAID (1999)

Brittle public finances

The relatively small size of Pacific island economies and the low population density and income levels tend to limit the range of tax instruments available to governments to raise revenue. Yet there are heavy demands on governments to fund development expenditure for essential infrastructure and other services, such as education and health. Thus, public finances of Pacific island economies tend to be stretched and rely heavily on foreign aid and excessive government borrowings from the central bank[11]. Despite periodic attempts to constrain the budget deficit, governments of island economies have generally failed to apply the necessary fiscal discipline needed to consolidate public finances by controlling unsustainable budget deficits. Fiscal imbalances are usually compounded by a lack of clear expenditure priorities by governments, with the result that scarce funds are often squandered on ill-conceived development projects (unfortunately supported at times by well-intentioned aid donors).

Narrow tax base encourages reliance on inefficient trade taxes

These economies have tended to have a narrow tax base due to their low levels of development, including the large informal sector located largely in remote rural areas, as well as their weak capacity in tax administration. Consequently, direct taxes on income (company and personal) and consumption that encounter collection and other administrative difficulties are supplemented by heavy reliance on trade taxes, including tariffs and export taxes. In PNG, for example, taxes on international trade,

---

[11] Recent reform to the Central Bank Act to restrict government borrowing to K100 million in any rolling 12-month period should help curtail fiscal irresponsibility. However, its success will depend on how effectively this limit is enforced. For example, previous legislative limits on new government borrowings in any year from the central bank of 10% of the estimated ordinary budgetary revenues, and of 20% on the stock of year-end debt, were generally ineffective. Similar legislative caps on central bank credit to government in the Solomon Islnads have also had only limited success.

predominantly import tariffs and export taxes, raised some 28% of government tax revenue in 1998. In the Solomon Islands, trade taxes, especially tariffs in recent years, have accounted for over half of government tax revenue. However, trade taxes are widely recognized to be an inefficient means of collecting government revenue. The economy would benefit if they were replaced by less-distorting taxes, such as direct income taxes once collection costs are brought down to reasonable levels, and/or a general consumption tax that applies equally to imported and domestically-produced goods. This means tariff and tax reforms are inextricably linked, since the former reduces government finances while the latter can enhance them. Papua New Guinea demonstrated this with the introduction on 1 July 1999 of a 10 per cent value-added tax (VAT) that provided the revenue for substantial across-the-board tariff reductions.

Budgetary processes also tend to be weak

Pacific island economies suffer from poor budgetary processes. Expenditure checks and controls are inadequate. Budgets in practice are rarely met, being based typically on overly optimistic revenue projections.

Public expenditure must match revenue constraints

All governments face revenue constraints, and ultimately there is no alternative to good fiscal planning than ensuring that governments live 'within their means' and spend only what is sustainable. Excessive public debt to finance budget deficits places upward pressures on interest rates and 'crowds out' the private sector. As well, such deficits flow through into larger external trade deficits that are often associated with accelerating inflation and an appreciation in the country's real exchange rate, thereby exposing governments to further lobbying pressure from domestic industries to provide more protection against imports. The PNG Government moved quickly on obtaining office in 1999 to redress fiscal imbalances, an essential pre-requisite for re-engaging dialogue with the IMF and the World Bank in support of PNG's reform programme.

Privatization can reduce wasteful public expenditure and raise efficiency

Ample evidence exists in Pacific island economies that governments have not used the financial resources available to them as effectively as they might. Such resources have been squandered by governments attempting to do things that would be best left to the private sector. For example, numerous island nation governments have been directly involved in commercial ventures, often jointly with private sector participants, with disastrous consequences in many cases. Thus, the Government's proper role needs to be re-defined, and in this context commercialization and privatization of state-owned enterprises can make an important contribution to releasing scarce budgetary funds needed for public investment. Most island economies are embarking on such programs, but with mixed success. In the case of PNG, the strategy developed is beginning to be put in place, so time will tell how successful it is. These arrangements will only work, however, if markets are also made competitive — competition improves efficiency, but increasing the degree of competition involves more than simply changing ownership.

Public provision of essential infrastructure and other services has been neglected

The quality of PNG's infrastructure has deteriorated badly during the past decade. Of major concern is the deteriorating road transport system. This raises business costs and in many cases prevents the efficient distribution and marketing of agricultural produce. Moreover, public utility prices, such as electricity and communications, are generally seen by business to be high cost, especially in view of the sub-standard quality of the services provided by the utilities. Electricity outages are common in Port Moresby, for example. Other public services, such as education and health, also have deteriorated, including the physical condition of many hospitals, schools and other educational institutions.

Declining law and order problems hurt the PNG economy

PNG's economic growth, and recently that of the Solomon Islands and Fiji, has been retarded by chronic and worsening law and order problems. This imposes substantial direct costs on businesses in the form of greater security expenses, and seriously prevents the economy from working efficiently. It also creates a hostile business environment and is a major constraint to attracting essential foreign direct investment and the overseas visitors needed to develop a thriving tourist industry. It also raises costs of employing expatriates and other foreign personnel needed to fill the domestic skill shortages. A recent survey ranked crime and theft as the most serious obstacles for business, with law and order problems perceived to have increased over the past ten years along with concerns about bribery (INA 1999).

Costs of law and order are not confined to urban areas

Among the hardest-hit by the law and order problem are agricultural industries. Because most of the informal agricultural sector works on cash, the serious risk of theft in rural areas prevents buyers from purchasing crops. Moreover, security concerns have also contributed in rural areas to bank branches closing, and to people being unwilling to open stores. This therefore penalizes the agricultural sector and reduces incentives for growers to expand output and to market their produce. For example, it has been estimated that almost one-third of PNG's coffee crop in 1997 was not marketed due to law and order problems (Togolo 1998).

Inward-looking trade policies

High tariffs generally prevail

Despite their strong trade orientation, Pacific island economies have tended to provide selective protection against imports to special industries largely in an attempt to promote primary processing and other manufacturing. Such import protection has taken many forms, but the most common in recent years has been via high and escalating tariff structures that have applied much higher rates to processed than unprocessed products. For example, prior to the introduction in PNG of the tariff reduction program on 1 July 1999, applied MFN tariffs averaged on an unweighted basis 20%, but ranged from free to 125%.[12] Although these rates are now being phased

---

[12] Import bans and quotas were previously used to encourage domestic manufacturing industries, such as canned beef, sugar,

down, and currently average 9%, much higher rates of up to 95% still apply to certain processed products.

The situation is similar in the Solomon Islands and Fiji. In the Solomon Islands, MFN tariffs averaged 23% in 1998, but ranged as high as 70% on certain processed products. Although tariffs are lower in Fiji, averaging 12% in 1997, they range up to 80 %.

Explaining the poor economic performance of PNG and other island economies

The erratic economic performance of PNG and other Pacific island economies stems from a combination of factors that go well beyond the scope of this report. However, there is little doubt that while external shocks, such as adverse weather conditions and depressed world commodity prices, contributed to their malaise, respective governments are mainly to blame due to their economic mismanagement and costly policies. In PNG, for example, successive governments have not fundamentally reversed the poor level of economic governance and related institutional weaknesses. It is true that recent macroeconomic management in PNG has improved, but there is a long way to go in this and other key policy areas.

---

cement, vegetables, flour, batteries and canned mackerel. However, these were removed, mainly by the early 1990s, and converted to high, sometimes prohibitive tariff rates, ranging mostly from 30% to 80%, but with some higher rates. The import ban on canned beef was converted to a tariff of 55% in 1994, for example, and the ten-year ban on sugar was replaced with a tariff of 85% in 1997. Most-favoured-nation (MFN) tariffs are those applying to imports from other WTO members that are not subject to preferential tariff rates that might have been agreed bilaterally or regionally. (Higher tariffs could in principle be applied to imports from non-WTO members.)

Good governance and institutions are elusive, yet vital for growth ...

Many of the problems identified, such as the worsening law and order, the collapse of institutions and due government processes, along with decaying public facilities such as transport, electricity, telecommunications, health and education, are symptomatic of fundamental problems with how PNG is being governed and managed economically and politically. Correlated to this is the increasing policy instability that has occurred over recent years. Even if policy corrections are implemented, they need to be followed through to the end. Economic reforms will only work if sustained and credible, and cannot in an environment of policy instability characterized by sudden policy reversals. There is evidence in PNG that such instability and uncertainty is increasingly impeding business and investment (INA 1999). Such retardation can be closely linked to political instability since frequent changes in governments are often associated with a loss of policy continuity.

... and must be a high priority

Without the basic institutions and sound governance needed for a vibrant private sector, other reform efforts will achieve limited benefits at best. The private sector needs secure individual property rights, especially to land, impartial enforcement of property and contractual rights (and more generally law and order) as well as appropriate formal and informal codes of conduct if it is to flourish and function efficiently.

Economic reforms can create a demand for institutional development

One of the virtues of economic reforms, such as trade and investment liberalization, is that they can create an environment that raises the demand for such institutional development. However, if they are not accompanied by fundamental institutional and governance reforms, dislocation and the costs of economic restructuring are likely to be increased and the benefits of reform diminished. That is, a 'stop/start' approach to economic reforms will increase dramatically the adjustment costs induced by policy changes, while reducing the benefits.

Box 2.1: Norfolk Island's Success – Smallness and Remoteness no Barrier to Prosperity

Despite Norfolk Island being small (around 35 square kilometers) and geographically isolated, it is not a typical Pacific island economy. It is more prosperous than Australia – some estimates put its GDP per capita in the late 1990s at 70 per cent higher than in Australia, compared with being 40% below in 1952 and at parity in 1976. What then has been the key to this success?

Its success has been due to economic flexibility. The economy has been able to efficiently adjust to the booms and busts of various activities throughout its history.

Although tourism is currently its main industry, this was not always the case. Whaling was its first leading sector, accounting for 45% of GDP in the late 1890s. However, the industry declined due to falling world prices but revived again in the 1950s before being shut down due to the sudden decline in whale numbers. However, other growth industries filled the void left by whaling. Government expansion during the 1900s stimulated the economy; not by the government dominating private and public consumption, but by establishing basic infrastructure and integrating the economy much more with the world economy.

Land reform prior to WWI paved the way for agricultural development. The original landholding system that restricted the original settlers from selling land was dismantled and a lease system implemented as well as unrestricted sale of freehold property.

Box 2.1: Norfolk Island's Success – Smallness and Remoteness no Barrier to Prosperity (continued)

The lemon industry aided by duty free access to Australia following its territorial status in 1914, flourished from 1915 to 1921, ending abruptly due to the collapse of the Sydney market. Bananas grew rapidly during the 1920s following an export boom created by the decimation of the Queensland and New South Wales banana crop in the mid-1920s. Exports expanded by tenfold between 1924 and 1929.

However, banana production folded in the early 1930s following the return of the more competitive Australian crop. Agriculture turned to exporting oranges, bean seeds and passion fruit. By the late 1950s disease, weather, price instability and competition from Australia all contributed to the decline and eventual closure of the industry. Since the 1960s, the mainstay of the economy has been tourism. Export receipts from tourism grew from A$8.7 million in 1978 to A$41 million in 1996.

Thus, the economy has displayed great flexibility in resource use in the face of a changing external environment. The island's openness in supplying goods and services and in factor markets, such as land, enabled the clear transmission of international price signals to determine the allocation of resources (Threadgold 1988). Labour laws, other regulations, and taxes have been kept to a minimum. The land market has functioned effectively, and the island's government has not had the luxury of running budget deficits based on excessive public service expenditure or revenue collections.

Source: Duncan, Cuthbertson and Bosworth (1999).

Smallness and isolation are in themselves no barrier to growth, provided good policies prevail

Problems of isolation, small size and unfavourable climatic conditions are not sufficient to explain PNG's poor economic performance, nor that of its Pacific neighbours. Such factors cannot be changed, and hence it is important that policies be implemented that make the best of these 'givens' rather than tolerating poor economic performance because of them (Commonwealth Secretariat/World Bank 2000). The economic development of Norfolk Island provides a good example of how a small remote island with almost no natural resources can become wealthy with good policies (Box 2.1).

Status quo policies have clearly not worked

Unless such wide-ranging reforms are implemented, economic growth in PNG and other Pacific island economies will continue to be erratic and disappointing. Such reforms must come from within the countries, and are in their own best interests irrespective of international developments. Nevertheless, implementing such reforms involves tremendous challenges which governments may be reluctant to face either because of ignorance of the benefits of reform or because of the short-term political consequences of such reforms.

Overcoming such resistance to reforms within government and the community has always been an essential part of meeting this challenge. As the next chapter explains though, in recent years the stakes have risen: globalization has accelerated, raising not only the rewards from good economic governance but also the penalty for bad economic governance.

3

Implications of globalization for Pacific development strategies

Pervasive effects of globalization

The pervasive effects of the process of globalization are being felt in poorer economies at least as much as in richer ones. But whether they are net positive or net negative influences for a particular country depends very much on the quality of economic governance in that country. What is globalization? What are the recent contributors to its recent acceleration? And what are its implications for Pacific island economies?

What is globalization?

Globalization can be defined as the decline in transactions costs or barriers to doing business or otherwise interacting with people internationally. It enhances the integration of markets for goods, services, technology, ideas, capital and labour, thereby reducing global differences in prices for those products and factors. Both technological and governmental barriers raise the costs of conducting business across borders. Reductions in transport costs, the huge decline in communication and information costs, and cuts in tariff and non-tariff barriers to trade in goods, services, financial capital, and to some extent labour have accelerated globalization to an unprecedented speed that shows no sign of abating.

Globalization manifests itself not just in global merchandise trade growth ...

The extent and pace of globalization cannot be captured in a single statistic, but several provide partial indications of its magnitude. A standard indicator is the comparison between trade and GDP growth globally. While merchandise trade has grown faster than output for virtually all two-decade periods since the 1700s except between the two world wars, the gap has been larger in the 1990s than in any earlier period since the mid-nineteenth century. More than one-fifth of global output is now exported, double the proportion in the 1950s.

... but also accelerated investment and services trade
Annual outflows of foreign direct investment grew more than six-fold between 1983 and 1990, and continued to grow more than twice as fast as goods trade in the 1990s. Some two-thirds of this is in services, commercial presence by foreign suppliers in host markets being the main means of trading services globally. Intra-firm trade among multinational corporations (MNCs) is estimated to account for one-third of world trade, and another one-third is MNC trade with non-affiliates. During the 1990s, international portfolio investment has been growing equally as fast as foreign direct investment. In the last five years, the annual value of cross-border mergers and acquisitions has trebled, growing from US$100 billion to more than US$300 billion. Daily foreign exchange transactions now exceed global currency reserves, with international capital flows more than 50 times the value of international trade flows. The 1990s also saw an explosion in the world's capacity for electronic commerce. The number of telephone lines doubled; there was a 25-fold increase in the number of cellular phones; the number of personal computers quadrupled; and two-thirds of those PCs are expected to have internet access by 2001.

The technological dimension of globalization

The on-going digital revolution is rapidly lowering communication costs
There have been three major technological revolutions in transport and communication costs. The cost of transporting goods was lowered enormously by the steam engine, which created the railway and steamship. Steel hulls for ships and refrigeration further lowered the cost of ocean transport late last century, particularly for perishable goods. The telegraph helped too. The second technological revolution lowered substantially the cost of moving people. It was dominated, in the middle half of this century, by falling transport costs by road and air thanks to

mass production and associated services. Ocean freight rates (helped by containerization) and telephone charges also fell massively over this period. The third and on-going revolution in transport and communications is in digital technology. Aided by deregulation of telecom markets in many countries, it is lowering enormously long-distance communication costs and especially the cost of rapidly accessing and processing knowledge, information and ideas from anywhere in the world. A side effect of the Internet's expansion is the growth in the use of the English language. It has been claimed that there are now more people using English as a second language than there are people for whom it is a first language. This too is lowering costs of communicating between countries.

The governmental contribution to globalization

Globalization is aided by trade and investment liberalization...

The above developments have been reinforced by government decisions to liberalize trade and investment regimes. Following the protectionist inter-war period, this began with the lowering of import tariffs on manufactured goods traded between industrial economies. In the 1980s trade reform was followed by extensive liberalization of foreign exchange markets and of restrictions on capital flows, leading (with the help of new digital technologies) to the development of new financial instruments. At the same time many non-OECD countries — including China and ultimately the Soviet bloc began moving away from inward-looking to outward-oriented trade and investment policies. The 1980s also saw the deregulation of domestic markets in a growing number of countries, developing as well as developed, which reinforced the effects of deregulating transactions at national borders.

... which benefits mainly the countries undertaking reform

These reforms benefit most the countries making them, but they also benefit their trading partners. Hence as more countries open up and reform, the greater is the gain to other countries from doing likewise. In particular, they expand the opportunities for developing and transition economies to access goods and services markets, investment funds and technologies, thereby raising the pay-off to liberalizing economies. Those that have already done so have grown much faster than the rest, and have seen their incomes converge toward OECD income levels (see, e.g., Dollar 1992; Edwards 1993; Sachs and Warner 1995; and WTO (1998, pp. 62-63 for a bibliography). They have also seen the welfare of their poorest citizens improve at least as much as that of their other citizens (Dollar and Kraah 2000). More generally, openness not only boosts the efficiency of resource use and economic growth, but simple open trade regimes aid good governance: they reduce the opportunities for discretionary policies and hence for corruption and arbitrariness, and they offer a way of conserving skilled labour for the many other challenges of development, such as improved education and more-efficient administration (Winters 2000).

Dynamics of trade liberalization are fundamental to growth

The reasons for faster growth of more open economies have to do with the dynamics of trade liberalization, something which is not just an abstract idea from new trade and growth theory but one that is well supported empirically (USITC 1997). There is always the risk that the market-opening reforms of the post-war period and especially the past fifteen years could be reversed by governments as domestic political circumstances change. However, that risk has been contained by the GATT and, since 1995, the WTO.

A more integrated world economy is here to stay

Together with the technological revolution, these policy reforms have brought about a more-integrated global trading system, a much more-integrated global capital market, and more integrated firms as international transactions that formerly took place between independent entities are being internalized within single firms or corporate alliances. The increasing mobility of the productive assets of firms enables them to minimize their corporate income tax exposure by strategically locating their headquarters and using transfer pricing in their intra-firm international trade. It also encourages governments to compete for the presence of firms with regulatory reforms and investment incentives. On the one hand this could leave governments with less tax revenue to supply social policies at a time when the demand for such policies is rising with income growth. On the other hand, if the regulatory reform is growth-enhancing and includes the privatization of state-owned enterprises, government revenue could expand.

Globalized production offers locational flexibility

These technological and governmental revolutions have contributed increasingly to the scope to subdivide the processes of production and distribution into parts that can be relocated anywhere in the world according to ever-increasing changes in comparative advantages over time. That out-sourcing can be via various means including sub-contracting, licensing, joint ventures and direct foreign investment by multinational corporations.

Human capital is increasingly the key to productivity growth

The resulting productivity growth in industrial and service sectors is altering the key source of wealth of nations, which is moving ever-faster away from natural to human capital (that is, from raw materials and physical capital per worker to human skills and knowledge). In particular, wealth creation in future will depend especially on the ability to access and make productive use of the expanding stocks of knowledge and information, and to build on them through creative research and development. How well and how quickly people of different countries are able to do that will increasingly determine relative economic growth rates. But for all countries the extent and speed with which economic events abroad are transmitted to domestic markets will increase inexorably. Governments will have less and less capacity to isolate their economies from such trends as derivatives and electronic commerce have made clear in the cases of international financial flows and a widening range of traded goods and services.

The GATT/WTO's contribution to globalization

International constraints are an effective means of preventing market-opening reversals

History shows that the risk of market-opening being reversed is much more likely in the absence than in the presence of international constraints on national trade policy actions. Following WWI, efforts to restore liberal trade centred on international conferences but did not lead to renewed trade treaties with binding commitments to openness based on MFN. Then when recession hit in the late 1920s, governments responded with beggar-my-neighbour protectionist trade policies that drove the world economy into depression. The volume of world trade shrunk by one-quarter between 1929 and 1932, and its value fell by 40 per cent. And the first attempts to reverse that protection were discriminatory, as with the Ottawa Conference of 1932 that led to preferential tariffs on trade among members of the British Commonwealth.

Trade rules and binding commitments were needed

Out of the inter-war experience came the conviction that liberal world trade required a set of rules and binding commitments based on non-discriminatory principles. While there was not enough agreement to create an international trade organization, at least a General Agreement on Tariffs and Trade was signed by 23 large trading countries in 1947. The GATT provided not only a set of multilateral rules and disciplines but also a forum to negotiate tariff reductions and rules changes, plus a mechanism to help settle trade disputes. Eight so-called rounds of negotiations took place in the subsequent 46 years, the last one (the Uruguay Round) culminating in the 'interim' GATT Secretariat being converted into the World Trade Organization.

WTO's four key objectives

The GATT, and now even more so the WTO, contributes to but also responds to the demands of globalization in several crucial ways (Appendix 3). The WTO has four key objectives: to set and enforce rules for international trade; to provide a forum to negotiate and monitor trade liberalization; to improve policy transparency; and to resolve trade disputes. Apart from the transparency role, these were also the key objectives of its predecessor. But the WTO is much more comprehensive than the GATT. For example, GATT's product coverage in practice was confined mainly to manufactures (effectively not including textiles and clothing), whereas the WTO encompasses all goods (including sensitive farm products), services, capital to some extent, and ideas (intellectual property). As well, the new WTO has greatly strengthened trade policy review and dispute settlement mechanisms.

WTO benefits small economies more

GATT/WTO rules to govern international trade serve three main purposes. First, they help protect the welfare of small and weak nations against discriminatory trade policy actions of large and powerful nations. GATT Articles I (most-favoured-nation) and III (national treatment) promise that all WTO members will be given the same conditions of access to a particular country's market as the most favoured member, and all foreign suppliers will be treated the same as domestic suppliers. These fairness rules are fundamental to instilling confidence in the world trading system. In particular, they lower the risks that are associated with a nation's producers and consumers becoming more interdependent with foreigners — risks that otherwise could be used by a country as an excuse for not fully opening its borders.

WTO reduces the scope for large traders to exploit their monopoly power

Second, large economies have the potential to exploit their monopoly power by taxing their trade, but we know from trade theory that the rest of the world and the world as a whole are made worse off by such trade taxes. Thus, while each large economy might be tempted to impose trade taxes, the effect of lots of them doing so simultaneously may well be to leave most if not all of them worse off — not to mention the welfare reductions that would result in many smaller countries. Hence, the value of agreeing not to raise trade barriers and instead to 'bind' them in a tariff schedule at specified ceiling levels. This rule is embodied in GATT Article II, whereby WTO members are expected to limit trade only with tariffs and are obligated to continue to provide market access never less favourable than that agreed to in their tariff schedules. Again, the greater certainty that this tariff-binding rule brings to the international trading system adds to the preparedness of countries to become more interdependent and of business people to invest more.

WTO helps governments cope with vested interest groups

The third and perhaps most important contribution of multilateral rules disciplining trade policy is that they can help governments ward off domestic interest groups seeking special favours. This comes about partly via Article II, which outlaws the raising of bound tariffs, as well as via numerous other articles aimed at ensuring that non-tariff measures are not used as substitutes for tariffs. This benefit of the system is sometimes referred to as the 'Ullyses effect': it helps prevent governments from being tempted to 'sin', in this case to favour special interest groups at the expense of the rest of their economy.[13]

WTO contributes to trade certainty and predictability

While no-one would argue that the GATT rules have worked perfectly or have been applied without exception, they help ensure that the worst excesses are avoided. Also, they provide all countries with a means of multilaterally challenging any import restrictions imposed by trading partners that are thought to be inconsistent with WTO disciplines[14]. They therefore bring greater certainty and predictability to international markets, enhancing economic welfare in and reducing political tensions between nations.

---

[13] Petersmann (1991, p. 83) goes so far as to say that "the primary regulatory function of the GATT .... [is] the welfare-increasing resolution of *domestic* conflicts of interest *within* GATT member countries among individual producers, importers, exporters and consumers ." Similarly, Roessler (1985, p. 298) claims that "the principal function of the GATT as a system of rules is to resolve conflicts of interest within, not among, countries. The function of the GATT as a negotiating forum is to enable countries to defend the national interest not against the national interests of other countries but against sectional interests within their own and other countries."

[14] For example, the decision in 1999 by the US to apply restrictions on lamb imports from Australia under GATT 'safeguard' rules is being challenged in the WTO by Australia and New Zealand as being inconsistent with these provisions.

Consumers are not the only losers from import barriers

One of the clearest lessons from trade theory is that an economy unable to influence its international terms of trade cannot maximize its national income and economic growth without allowing free trade in all goods and services. Consumers lose directly from the higher domestic prices of importables, while exporters lose indirectly because import barriers cause the nation's currency to appreciate (there is less demand for foreign currency from importers) and raise the price of labour and other mobile resources. More-open economies also grow faster.

Governments restrict trade mainly for reasons of political economy

Why, then, do countries restrict their trade? Numerous reasons have been suggested, but almost all of them are found wanting (Corden 1997). The most compelling explanation is a political economy one. It has to do with the national income re-distributive feature of trade policies. The gains are concentrated in the hands of a few that are prepared to support politicians that favour protection. However, the losses are sufficiently small per consumer and export firm and are distributed sufficiently widely as to make it not worthwhile for those losers to get together to provide a counter-lobby, particularly given their greater free-rider problem in acting collectively.

Implications of globalization for Pacific island countries' policy choices

Globalization offers benefits to poorer countries, but also challenges

Greater openness of and interdependence between national economies provides wonderful opportunities for poorer economies, but it presents challenges. Globalization is raising the rewards to economies choosing good economic governance, but is also raising the cost to economies with poor economic governance. Just as financial capital can now flow into a well-managed economy more easily and quickly than ever before, so it can equally quickly be withdrawn if confidence in that economy's governance is shaken. The East Asian crisis during the late 1980s, and the two coups in Fiji, has demonstrated this all too clearly.

**Liberalization
increasingly a
part of good
governance**

Two aspects of good economic governance are especially worthy of mention in the wake of globalization: commitment to a liberal international trade and payments regime, and growth-enhancing domestic policies that are not sectorally biased. Together these will enable producers to take maximum advantage of new/prospective export opportunities.

Commitment to a liberal trade and payments regime

**A stable
trading
environment is
important**

The above suggests the first priority for a poor country seeking to achieve sustainable economic development is to practice good economic governance generally. In particular, it should commit to a permanently open international trade and payments regime underpinned by those institutions essential for private sector development, such as providing secure property rights (intellectual as well as physical). A long-term commitment to openness is more crucial now than ever. Otherwise, capital flows will be short-term, and susceptible to sudden withdrawal should confidence waver. It is for this reason, and because of the comprehensiveness of the Uruguay Round agreements, that liberal trade policy commitments under the WTO are so important. Potential investors value them because WTO commitments involve (a) legal bindings and (b) most-favoured-nation treatment by trading partners. The legal bindings mean a WTO member cannot return to a more protectionist regime by raising tariffs above the bound rates listed in the member's schedules of commitments. Nor does that member risk facing higher than MFN bound tariffs in exporting to its trading partners if they are WTO members.

**Investor
confidence is
enhanced by
WTO
membership**

The security of a stable trading environment instills a confidence in investors that is noticeably less in non-WTO countries. For such countries a key ingredient in achieving good economic governance is to seek speedy accession to the WTO. Already there are almost 140 members of the new organization, and 30 countries are in the process of undergoing accession. The WTO is thus approaching the status of a truly global trade organization, except for under-representation by two groups: the former centrally planned economies (CPEs) seeking to transform to market orientations, and some of the smallest and poorest economies[15]. Most of the CPEs not already members are seeking WTO accession, the most notable being China (whose accession would allow Chinese Taipei to join) and Russia. For the other group feeling marginalized, the world's smallest and least-developed countries, the cost of the accession process, and subsequently of maintaining a mission in Geneva that is large enough to cover the expanding number of items of key concern to them, is high when expressed in per capita terms.

Developing countries' concerns with WTO are being addressed

Efforts are being taken multilaterally and bilaterally to address these concerns of poor countries. For example, it has been recommended that the WTO should review the current accession process as it affects small states to see if the problems and costs faced by these economies can be reduced (IMF 2000). There is also a need to supplement the meager resources of these countries to facilitate their participation in trade negotiations. The WTO allows groups of small states to be represented collectively at discussions, and is seeking more funds from members to enhance its already substantial technical assistance programmes. The Forum and Commonwealth Secretariats could play significant roles in enhancing WTO representation by Pacific island economies. ACP states, including these economies, also benefit from the bureau funded in Geneva by the EU to facilitate negotiations with the WTO.

---

[15] Of the 48 UN designated least-developed countries, 29 are WTO members and a further 10 countries have observer status, of which 6 countries are currently undergoing accession. Some 23 countries have Geneva-based representation.

The trend among developing countries is to open their economies

To what extent are less-advanced economies opening up to trade? The answer is that many are opening up substantially — including several in Africa. Some of those reform programs have been adopted with reluctance as conditions for receiving IMF or World Bank loans, while others have been unconditional unilateral decisions. Until they are bound under the WTO, though, there is a risk of back-sliding in the future. Furthermore, tariffs need to be bound at levels close to applied rates to be taken seriously, unlike during the Uruguay Round when many developing countries, including Pacific island economies, committed to ceiling bindings at well above the level of applied rates.

Growth-enhancing domestic policies that are not sectorally biased

Domestic policies are wasteful if not sectorally neutral

The extent to which liberalizing one's own trade and payments regime and securing greater market access opportunities for one's exports boosts a developing country's economic growth depends importantly also on the domestic policy environment. Sound, predictable, stable macroeconomic and taxation policies that are not sectorally biased are essential. Uruguay Round reforms abroad will make agricultural and textile/clothing exports more profitable for many developing countries. Trade liberalization at home will tend to reinforce that, because many developing economies have traditionally protected manufacturing at the expense of primary production — a pro-urban bias.

Traditional protectionist policies tend to discriminate against rural activities

Those past trade and other urban policy biases discouraged investment in infrastructure and human capital in rural areas. Realizing the productive potential of the rural sector requires major upgrading of essential rural infrastructure to lower the transactions costs of doing business, plus it requires investment in the people involved. The crucial infrastructure includes rural roads, electricity, telecommunications and radio transmission, so that costs of transport, communications and information (about market conditions, new technologies and the like) become more affordable. Investments in these items probably will be more expensive per capita than in urban areas, but that needs to be weighed against the net long-term benefits from expanding output faster from rural areas.

Investments in human capital boost growth and make adjustment easier

The crucial investments in people include basic schooling (for both sexes) and health services, as well as agricultural research and extension. All the empirical evidence points to the social rates of return from such public investments being high in developing countries even when price and trade policies discriminate heavily against the rural sector; hence they are likely to be even higher as and when those policies are reformed. If/where those social rates of return are significantly above private rates, a case might be made for government subsidies. The case is especially strong for human capital investments in rural areas. Such investments not only raise farm incomes and so reduce the social and economic problems of 'urban drift' associated with farmers leaving agriculture; they also increase the prospects for non-farm jobs in rural areas. In both respects, the social tensions that are inevitably associated with rapid economic growth and structural change are lessened.

4

Policy reforms to boost development of the Pacific islands

International experience shows that openness is the key to growth and poverty alleviation ...

It is widely recognized that major structural changes in PNG and other Pacific island economies are needed to improve their economic efficiency and growth performance. Major impediments to those structural adjustments are distortionary trade and investment policies. This is now being widely recognised, thanks to the now-overwhelming body of evidence supporting the idea of mutual interdependence between economic growth and openness to international trade and investment (Dollar 1992; Edwards 1993). A particularly telling study found that open economies grew on average three times faster than closed economies (Sachs and Warner 1996). The study looked at the performance of eight always open and forty always closed economies from 1966 to 1990. Although the precise links are less clear, there is also strong evidence that openness can lead to reductions in poverty and income disparity (Dollar and Kraay 2000; Ben-David, Nordstrom and Winters 2000), and to enhanced economic and social development generally (Winters 2000)[16].

... even though some may suffer in the adjustment period

This is not to say that such policy reforms will make absolutely everybody better off. There will always be a few losers from structural adjustments that accompany economic growth, regardless of whether those adjustments are induced by changes in technology, tastes and

---

[16] Evidence from Chile's liberalization policies, for example, indicates that although income inequality worsened initially, it subsequently returned to pre-reform levels at vastly higher average incomes and lower poverty levels.

preferences, international terms of trade, domestic or trade policies. But the best way to deal with that concern is to ensure appropriate tax and social welfare policies are in place, rather than to avoid trade and investment policy reforms. Avoiding reform does not remove the need for adjustment, it simply delays incurring that one-off adjustment cost and in the meantime continues to impose on-going costs year after year (in terms of foregone efficiency gains) on the society.

East Asia is not the only open region

The income growth in many East Asian economies over recent decades that has been associated with a high degree of openness that fuelled rapid export growth and investment rates is well recognized. But there are also examples of successful liberalization efforts in small countries that have similar features to PNG, such as Mauritias, Trinidad and Tobago and Jamaica (Box 4.1). In Trinidad and Tobago and Jamaica, for example, strong trade policy reforms in the early 1990s were followed by improved export and overall economic growth, following lack-lustre performance during a long period of inward-looking policies (Findlay and Wellitz 1993; Rajapatirana 1997). In the South Pacific, Samoa currently is undergoing such reforms with promising results (Box 4.2).

Open developing economies do very well

An important reason as to why openness to trade and investment helps developing country economies grow is that it facilitates transfer of technology and know-how from developed countries. Developing countries must take advantage of this 'catch up' factor that openness provides if they are to maximize growth in the early stages of their development. Of course the technology needs to be appropriate given the countries' relative factor prices and factor endowments, so often that would preclude the latest skill- and capital-intensive technologies.

Box 4.1: The Liberalization Experience of Trinidad and Tobago and Mauritius

These WTO members have many economic similarities with PNG and other Pacific island nations. They are also small lowly populated island economies subject to similar climatic variations, limited output and market opportunities. However, while still heavily reliant on a few major products and concentrated export markets, they have successfully diversified in the face of external commercial pressures. Trinidad and Tobago remains a resource-based economy heavily dependant on oil and gas, but now process more downstream products. Manufactured goods, led by petrochemicals and iron and steel, accounted for almost 40% of exports in 1996 compared to 5% in 1980. Similarly, Mauritius has diversified away from sugar, which now accounts for 25% of exports — down from 90% of exports in 1970 — into clothing, tourism and, more recently, offshore financial services. The service sector accounts for over one-half of GDP and one-third of total exports. Both countries depend heavily on a few export markets; about one-half of Trinidad and Tobago's exports are to the US while 70% of merchandise exports from Mauritius are to the EU under Lome preferences, mainly on clothing and sugar.

Both economies have recently experienced strong growth turnarounds. Following the 1973-82 oil boom, per capita incomes in Trinidad and Tobago declined to pre-1973 levels, but has grown by 3-4% annually since 1995. Mauritius recorded exceptional growth during the 1980s, with per capita income almost tripling from 1980-93. Both economies have become more resilient to external shocks and appear better placed to handle changing economic circumstances. Despite their dualistic nature, leading sector growth has contributed to the rest of the economy. Export growth underpinned by strong foreign investment has been essential to their development.

Box 4.1: The Liberalization Experience of Trinidad and Tobago and Mauritius (continued)

It is impossible to fully explain their improved performances, Nevertheless, structural economic reforms, underpinned by trade and investment liberalization, and improved macro-stabilization policies have contributed enormously along with political stability and good governance—growth in both cases has followed or coincided with market-opening policies. Improved stabilization policies and fundamental structural reforms in Trinidad and Tobago since 1994, including tariff reductions, privatization, investment liberalization and flexible exchange rates, have attracted substantial foreign investment, particularly in the energy sector. Mauritius's trade and investment regime was also extensively liberalized and prudent macro-economic policies adopted, including exchange rate flexibility. Tariffs are now the main instrument of protection in both nations.

Trade and tax reforms have been intertwined to remove their traditional dependence on trade taxes, including tariffs and export taxes. Trinidad and Tobago no longer depends on trade taxes for government revenue; tariff revenue now accounts for below 4% of government revenue, due to the increased importance of other taxes, such as VAT, income taxes and royalties. Mauritius has also taken steps, including the introduction of a VAT as an alternative to tariff revenue which previously accounted for about one-half of government revenue. Exports have been liberalized, and Mauritius no longer taxes sugar exports.

Although regional liberalization has been important — for Trinidad and Tobago mainly via membership of the Caribbean Community and Common Market (CARICOM) and for Mauritius primarily as a member of the Common Market for Eastern and Southern Africa (COMESA) this has not been at the expense of MFN liberalization. Moreover, while these economies have received preferential access to export markets, such as the EU under Lome, they have developed a capacity to adapt to changing market conditions.

Source: WTO (1995 and 1998c).

Box 4.2: Samoan Trade Reforms

Samoa adopted comprehensive trade reforms in 1998 that provide important lessons to other pacific island economies. The tariff structure was simplified from eight to five different rates, and duties lowered generally across-the-board to a maximum rate of 20 per cent, down from 60 per cent. Customs administration is also being rationalized, including the establishment of WTO valuation procedures. Tariff exemptions and concessions that were widespread and applied on a discretionary basis were also largely revoked. These tariff reforms were financed by the introduction in 1994 of a 10 per cent value-added goods and services tax (VAGST) at a time when the government was facing severe budgetary pressures

The Government is committed to structural and sectoral reforms based on good governance. It intends achieving this by making Samoa a more enterprise-based and competitive economy by developing a strong and diversified private sector. These reforms stemmed largely out of desperation. The economy had suffered a number of setbacks in the 1990s resulting from exogenous climatic and other factors as well as large commercial losses by state-owned enterprises.

The Government had adopted a comprehensive reform program covering tax, corporatization, tariffs, finance, macro-economic stabilization and monetary stability. This has meant that the gains and losses have tended to be widespread and individually small. Pressures created by informal imports from American Samoa eroded formal import systems and made tariff protection impractical. This coincided with a growing public recognition that high import tariffs were counter-productive. The Government also involved stakeholders in the discussions to generate support from the private sector and the general public.

Source: Duncan, Cuthbertson and Bosworth (1999).

That can be an advantage for developing countries though, since more-advanced economies often have second-hand, labour-intensive machinery available for much less than the new price of the machinery replacing it in the high-wage country.

Economic gains stem from exploiting comparative advantage and improving productivity

Living standards depend upon resource endowments and productivity levels. Trade liberalization improves productivity by enabling economies to focus more on what they can produce best according to their comparative advantage, given their endowments of natural resources, labour and capital. This is the basic economic principle underpinning international trade. Countries will gain from trade by specializing in products in which they have a comparative advantage (in which they produce relatively 'best' in terms of comparative cost), and importing those in which they have a comparative disadvantage. Because it is relative domestic costs that determine comparative advantage, all nations will be better off producing some goods and not others by specializing and trading. They will benefit from importing even those goods in which they have an absolute advantage − that is, they are the world's lowest cost producer − provided they are even more efficient, or have a greater absolute advantage, in producing other goods. All countries will have comparative advantages and disadvantages in some products, and all can therefore benefit from trade.

Trade liberalization yields productivity gains

Productivity improves when trade is increased. Extra competitive pressures on previously protected industries, and new technical know how from new foreign investment opportunities, can raise productivity and create higher growth. Empirical evidence suggests that such gains can be very significant (Stockel, Tang and McKibbin 1999; Stockel and Corbett 1999; Frankel and Romer 1999).

Better to let competitive markets 'discover' comparative advantage

The policy challenge is to ensure that countries are able to follow their pattern of comparative advantage as it evolves through time. This is best assured by allowing competitive markets to determine production, consumption and trade. Given appropriate institutions and policies, markets can deliver efficient results and ensure that outputs and inputs are supplied at minimum costs. The determinants of comparative advantage are varied and complex, and result from the complicated interaction of many markets that change in the course of economic development at home and abroad (as described in Appendix 4). Competitive markets boost productivity and open markets are an efficient means of exposing domestic producers to competition. Without such competition, domestic producers may be able to survive — but they will be inefficient by world standards and so will the level and growth of national income.

Pay off from trade reforms is higher with complementary investment liberalization

Without openness to foreign direct investment, a smaller volume of the financial resources needed to exploit areas of comparative advantage will be available domestically. That is, trade liberalization will develop more-efficient industries easier if foreign investment restrictions are also removed. Trade and investment reform are thus closely linked and are needed together if firms, and hence countries, are going to benefit fully from the opportunities provided by globalization. Although liberalizing foreign investment without trade reforms may attract foreign firms seeking to operate behind 'tariff walls', this may well be counter-productive since such investment will tend to be in highly protected activities that are unlikely to be internationally competitive and hence incapable of exporting without government subsidies.

Open policies benefit all economies, including small states

The relevance of open trade and investment policies for improving economic performance applies equally to all countries, irrespective of their size. While small states do present special developmental problems that need to be taken into account, these states must nevertheless adapt, indeed transform, their economies to secure the benefits of globalization and the increasingly open global trading environment (IMF 2000). Open trade policy is best viewed as part of sound overall economic management and development strategies for small states as it is with all developing countries (and developed countries for that matter).

Can governments do better than markets?

Trade policy is often used as industry policy in the belief that governments know more than firms

Import barriers, such as tariffs, are often applied by governments in an attempt to promote industrialization. This view is sometimes premised on the belief that governments should actively intervene in the market to determine areas of comparative advantage. It presupposes, however, that governments are better than market forces at identifying efficient activities. Experience suggests that is almost always not the case, however. Hence, governments should refrain from such activities.

Can governments outperform markets?

This frequently asked question lies at the core of resistance to trade liberalization. There has been no shortage of attempts by governments throughout the world to intervene in markets to establish 'preferred outcomes'. This is certainly true of PNG and some other Pacific island economies. Governments consistently intervene, despite there being no evidence to suggest they are able to consistently outperform the market.

Firms get it wrong sometimes, but governments get it wrong more often

Choosing successful outcomes that would have been selected by the market in any event is not alone sufficient to justify government intervention. For governments to be successful, they would need to consistently pick promising industries for development that would have been missed by the private sector. Clearly, it is difficult to identify such activities in practice. However, what is observable are the number of failures selected by governments in Pacific island economies and elsewhere. This demonstrates that governments are generally inept in trying to 'second guess' markets. That should not be surprising, since governments generally focus on development of industries that would not otherwise grow, and hence their commercial viability is nearly always bound to incur high risks.

Assisting industries involves the government trying to 'pick winners'

Governments often justify their intervention on their ability to pick winners. But it is difficult to see why governments are consistently in a better position to do so than the private sector. If governments base their decisions on having access to superior information, then the most efficient outcome is not for the government to support the targeted industry, but rather to correct whatever the failure is in the market for information, to ensure that the private sector can access the same information. Moreover, the likelihood that governments would be better than the private sector at picking winners is even further undermined in Pacific island economies where governments have very limited human resources. In any case, those limited bureaucratic resources would be best spent on providing the essential public goods required for sustainable development.

Infant industries that need government nurturing seem to never grow up

Governments often protect new or 'infant' industries to allow them to operate initially without competition so they can expand and become established commercially before being exposed to competition. This presupposes that one day the industry will become competitive without protection. Experience suggests, however, that such industries requiring assistance 'at birth' require long-term government support and rarely mature into efficient industries that have a comparative advantage. Moreover, in small markets such as those in the Pacific island economies, where other domestic suppliers are unlikely and the extent to which economies of scale can be realized from home sales is extremely limited, arguments supporting infant industry protection against imports would appear even weaker[17].

---

[17] For a powerful critique of each of the standard arguments for infant industry protection, and suggested rankings of policy instruments that would be far superior to trade measures for dealing with each concern, see Corden (1997, Ch. 8).

Matching overseas protection or subsidies is counter-productive

Governments often provide protection to offset against trade-distorting foreign subsidies or protectionist policies that distort world markets. As harmful as these foreign subsidies might be for efficient domestic producers, providing counter protection only increases the economic costs at home and abroad of such interventions. The most appropriate longer-term response by countries adversely affected by these arrangements is to increase their own productivity and efficiency so as to compete with the subsidized product (the so-called 'level playing field' argument). This at first may appear counter-intuitive, but is especially relevant to small Pacific island economies that have scarce public funds.

Sugar production assistance in PNG is an example

The PNG sugar industry is a case in point. The high tariff protection is claimed by the industry to be necessary in part to counteract the depressing effects on international sugar prices of distorting protectionist policies by other major sugar producers, such as the EU and US. However, while such policies by overseas producers should be removed (something the WTO membership and sugar-exporting countries in particular seek to achieve), it is impossible for PNG to become better off by highly protecting its own sugar industry. Simply because other governments select bad policies is no reason for PNG to follow suit. On the contrary, since PNG would be a sugar importer in the absence of protection, it should welcome those low international sugar prices as that improves the country's terms of trade and in particular the welfare of its consumers (both food processors and households). Of greatest importance is to use the nation's resources most efficiently, and selectively assisting sugar production is likely to be inconsistent with this national goal. While it may increase employment in the sugar industry, less people are employed elsewhere — including in more internationally competitive industries — as a result. What determines domestic efficiency is not the level of assistance provided home industries relative to foreign producers, but its level of assistance compared with other domestic industries. Providing industry assistance that necessarily becomes selective since governments can never assist all activities equally, therefore always trades-off the interests of one industry against another. Efforts to justify such selective assistance on grounds of employment generation or 'multiplier effects' are therefore misguided since all activities, if assisted, will generate these results. But why should one industry be assisted and not others?

The PNG reform program

The need for reform is being recognised

Trade and investment liberalization is increasingly being recognized domestically as fundamental to creating a more flexible and efficient PNG economy. Hence the focus on them in this report, because that is the Pacific country where the WTO and APEC are likely to have their main policy impact. However, trade and investment reforms alone will do less than they might unless other essential reforms are made simultaneously to promote good governance and institutional arrangements. Governance is concerned with the role of the state and the institutions established to manage development. Good governance requires a predictable, open, and enlightened policymaking system that is accountable and functions within transparent rules of law that are effectively enforced.

Tariff reforms

A tariff reduction program is in place in PNG

After several delays, PNG implemented a major across-the-board tariff reduction program on 1 July 1999 as part of its on-going structural adjustment program. Maximum MFN bound tariffs were reduced immediately from 125% to 55%, apart from higher rates of up to 95% being maintained for certain sensitive products including sugar, tinned mackerel and plywood. Average (unweighted) tariffs fell to 9% and are being phased down to 5% by 2006 when the highest tariff rate will be 40%. Once completed, the tariff structure will comprise just four rates: free, 15%, 25% and 40%. The tariff reductions were financed primarily by the introduction of a 10% value added tax on goods and services.

Lower, but still high, effective protection rates prevail

This program should improve economic efficiency by providing a more neutral tariff structure and lower levels of net or effective protection (Box 4.3). It is estimated that effective rates of protection for manufacturing (including food processing) have fallen from an average in 1992 of 160% — ranging from 90% to 105% in 1998 prior to the reforms — to between 67% and 80% in 1999. These are estimated to fall further to the 42% to 50% range at the end of the current tariff reduction program. This will help reduce the discriminatory impact that the tariff has had on PNG's major agricultural export crops of coffee, oil palm and cocoa (WTO 1999). These activities received negative effective assistance and were thus being heavily penalized under the previous tariff structure (Table 4.1).

Tariffs on imports tax PNG exports

One of the main obstacles to exports in PNG is the high level of import tariffs. That has both direct and indirect effects on other industries. Relatively high tariffs on manufactured products can directly raise input costs to efficient agricultural exporters who cannot pass on the cost increases because they are price takers in world markets. Much more important than that direct effect is an indirect one: they cause an appreciation of the exchange rate, which lowers the price of exports in domestic currency terms, and they raise the price to exporters of inter-sectorally mobile factors of production, most notably labour. In these ways PNG's protectionist policies that provide high levels of assistance to industries in which PNG has no comparative advantage, such as sugar, cement, plywood and mackerel canning, are penalizing traditional competitive export crops of coffee, cocoa, copra and oil palm. Lowering tariffs will therefore remove the anti-export bias inherent in PNG's tariff structure.

Table 4.1: Effective rates of protection for selected activities, PNG, early 1990s

(per cent)

Commodity/product	Effective rate of protection
A. Agriculture	
Sugar	110
Tea	-4
Cocoa/copra	-4 to -14
Cocoa/balsa	-2
Coffee	-1 to -22
Oil palm	-2 to zero
B. Fishing	
Fishing	-23
C. Livestock	
Meat	-11 to 22; negative value added
D. Manufacturing	
Food processing	106 to 228; negative value added
Coffee processing	30
Tobacco products	80
Chemicals	-134
Soaps and cosmetics	91; negative value added
Paint	36
Matches	35
Packaging	970
Printing	67
Clothing	53 to 62
Tyres	43
Steel products	32 to 49
Jewellery	117

. *Note:* See Box 4.3 for definitions and explanations.
. *Source:* REPIM Ltd (1996).

Manufacturing protection has not generated industrial- ization

Efforts to use trade policy to encourage industrialization have generally had little success in PNG and other island economies, despite the government agreeing to provide special protection on certain products, initially in the form of import bans, and more recently since the mid-1990s by high tariffs.

Sugar, for example, continues to receive high protection that assists its production ...

The government initially granted Ramu Sugar an import ban in 1984 to establish a sugar cane production and processing complex in the Ramu Valley (Box 4.4). The ban was subsequently converted to a prohibitive tariff in 1997 that was set at 85% in 1998. Because of a non-public government agreement with Ramu Sugar, which is 49% government owned, tariff reduction commitments under the program have been backloaded and so tariffs will fall from 82% currently to 70% by 2005 and to 40% from 2006. Thus, sugar production will continue to receive very high assistance for some years. The sugar industry's competitive position is weak because of an unsuitable climate, which lowers sugar content of cane and encourages pests, and from lack of economies of scale because of small throughput of the milling factory of some 40,000 to 50,000 tonnes annually. Current indications are that the survival of Ramu sugar will need a tariff of substantially above the long term rate of 40% if it is to remain viable. Thus, there is the possibility of closure of Ramu sugar (as would be in the national interest if it cannot be competitive without a tariff of any size, let alone one as high as 40%). That would have major structural adjustment implications for the Ramu workers and the community, of course.

... but at the direct expense of food processors and consumers

These one-off adjustment costs, however, need to be considered in relation to the benefits that will forever flow afterwards to the economy. One source of benefits would come from downstream food processors and consumers having access to better-quality sugar at much lower — about half — existing prices. Sugar is a major input into foodstuffs and beverages, and hence reducing sugar protection will be to their benefit. Downstream sugar users, such as the breweries, have been critical not only of the high price but also of the variable quality of Ramu sugar.

Many processors must further treat sugar prior to using it for processing, an additional cost imposed on them by sugar protection.

What if those food processors also were to be protected?

If the food processors and breweries are themselves protected from import competition, as Table 4.1 suggests, it might be argued that this more or less offsets the higher cost of inputs such as protected sugar. In that case, reducing sugar protection may add to rather than reduce resource misallocation since mobile resources could move to even more protected activities. This is not an argument for avoiding sugar reform though. On the contrary, it simply illustrates the general point that the more distorted an economy, the more important it is to have across-the-board liberalization so as to ensure that resources do move to more-efficient activities.

Food import substitution policies are a poor recipe for a vibrant food-exporting sector ...

The PNG Government's policies have been aimed at substituting food imports with local production, especially for poultry and rice in addition to sugar. These were said to be justified on the grounds of increasing food self sufficiency, regional employment (as with Ramu), and reducing the drain of food imports on foreign exchange. However, such policies not only raise food prices (doubling them in the case of sugar, compared with import prices[18]), but also effectively tax potential agricultural exporters and cause the sector's resources to be diverted towards lower-value crops than would prevail under freer markets (Gibson 1997). In addition, these policies discriminate against the informal agricultural sector that receives little government support, including cash cropping of traditional food items such as bananas, sweet potatoes, cassava and taro. Hence, the net effect on food self sufficiency and foreign exchange savings/earnings may well be negative rather than positive, and there is no reason to assume that the highly protected activities would employ more people than the currently less protected ones.

---

[18] Gibson 1993. Although these estimates were made well before 1997 when the sugar import ban was converted to a tariff, they are still relevant given the high rates, inirtially of 85% and currently 82%.

... and impose an inequitable tax on poor consumers

Higher food prices from tariffs and other forms of protection tax households regressively by hurting poor consumers the most. It has been estimated, for example, that the poorest one-tenth of households pay a sugar tax from protection equivalent to 3.2% of the value of sugar consumed, compared to a tax of only 0.6% paid by the wealthiest one-tenth of households (Gibson 1997). Thus, removing such inequitable taxes by dismantling trade barriers on staple items, such as food, will directly help alleviate poverty by raising the real incomes of the poorest households.

Tariff escalation remains

Despite the significant benefits of the reform program to date, tariff escalation remains substantial in PNG and will do so even when the phased reductions are completed. The highest rate to be in place in 2006, 40% (on mainly processed products) exceeds considerably the rates on raw materials and other inputs of either zero or 15%. Escalating tariffs apply much higher effective assistance for processed products than for unprocessed materials. This is mainly justified on the grounds of encouraging downstream value added processing. However, encouraging such activities by providing high protection is counter-productive since those activities are only worthwhile pursuing if they add more value — when measured at international prices — than what would otherwise be produced. Moreover, that protection may penalize efficient agricultural producers of unprocessed foodstuffs that have considerable export potential by encouraging them to focus on inward-looking processed activities that cater mainly for the domestic market.

Box 4.3: Effective Rates of Protection

The effective rate of protection (or assistance) is a standard tool used to measure the assistance provided individual domestic activities due to trade barriers applying to competing imports, such as tariffs and quotas. Whereas tariff levels on outputs indicate its gross or nominal assistance, the effective rate measures the activity's net assistance by taking into account the benefits and costs of protection on both output and inputs, related to the activity's value added. Thus, tariffs on outputs assist domestic producers by enabling them to sell in the home market at a higher price, while tariffs on inputs penalize users by raising their domestic (and import) price. It is given by the formula:

Effective rate (%)

$$= \frac{\text{value added with assistance} - \text{value added without assistance}}{\text{value added without assistance}} \times \frac{100}{1}$$

Since value added is measured at world prices, it is possible for it to be negative. This means that when valued at world prices, the cost of the activity's inputs exceed its output price. These activities are only maintained by government assistance, and thereby receive very high levels of support. They are highly inefficient users of the community's resources, which would be improved if the products were instead imported.

The effective rate estimates presented in Table 4.1 for PNG provide a useful indicator of the likely adverse effects on economic efficiency of the tariff structure. These estimates pre-date the July 1999 tariff reductions. Nevertheless, they are still useful since the tariff reforms are likely to have tended to reduce absolute rather than relative effective rate levels since it is mainly the same industries that continue to receive the highest tariff protection. Indeed, disparities in effective rate levels may have widened, at least in the short term, on products that received favourable treatment involving the maintenance of high tariff protection, while benefiting immediately from zero tariffs on basic and intermediate inputs.

One study on effective assistance concluded that:

- Export products were negatively assisted;
- Food processing was generally highly protected, with many having negative value added at world prices;
- Although the livestock sector enjoyed high tariffs, it operated in a competitive environment that ensured that the benefits of protection were not used;
- While steel products have a lower range of protection, other intermediate inputs such as packaging and paint exhibited high levels of protection; and
- The range of protection on final goods was wide.

Source: WTO (1999).

Box 4.4: Sugar Production in PNG

PNG embarked on establishing a national sugar industry in 1982 aimed at achieving sugar self-sufficiency and contributing to national development. To achieve this, the Government established a monopoly domestic sugar producer, Ramu Sugar Limited (RSL), initially protected by a ten-year import ban and now by a prohibitive tariff of above 80%. The government is the largest single shareholder of RSL holding a 48.8 per cent interest. A private company manages RSL.

The sugar price is administratively set by the Government according to an agreed pricing formula whereby the price is adjusted at 6-monthly intervals by the consumer price index, subject to a maximum yearly increase of 8 per cent. The initial agreement was for three years from 1985, but was extended. Despite the high levels of 'infant industry protection' provided by the monopoly arrangements, RSL has performed poorly. In its first 11 years, it made notable profits in only three years. No dividends were paid in the first 10 years. In hindsight, the original feasibility study was too optimistic. It concluded that a project producing around 40,000 tonnes annually would be commercially viable at a minimum world price of US$0.155 cents per pound, corresponding to an import parity ('into store, Lae') price of US$0.34 per pound (in 1982 dollars). At that time, sugar prices were projected to rise rapidly. However, shortly after Ramu commenced production in the early 1980s, the world sugar price sank to historically low levels, and import parity pricing for Ramu sugar had to be abandoned. Between 1988 and 1998, the world price of sugar varied from US$0.08 to US$0.15 per pound, and averaged US$0.11 per pound. The domestic market for sugar is currently about 35,000 tonnes annually and around 7,000 tonnes is exported under quota to the US each year. In addition, the industry produces both ethanol, which is blended with petrol by major oil companies, and potable alcohol for export and domestic sales.

Box 4.4: Sugar Production in PNG (continued)

It has been estimated that, while the import prohibition was in place, the domestic price of sugar was on average double world levels. The ban was replaced with a prohibitive tariff from 1997 of 85% that was reduced to its current level of 82% in 1999. Under the new tariff reduction program, duties are supposed to be phased down in the first half of this decade, but they have been back-loaded and so have yet to occur. The largest tariff cut for sugar is scheduled to occur in 2006 when the rate will fall from 70% to 40%. Thus, the change from an import prohibition to a prohibitive tariff will have had only a small impact in reducing industry assistance up to 2005. Meanwhile, the domestic price of sugar remains above world levels to the extent of the existing tariff, that is, by 82%.

It has been estimated using Domestic Resource Costs and other techniques that PNG does not have a comparative advantage in sugar production. This would continue to be the case under the most optimistic scenarios in which world sugar prices would rise following liberalization of the global market. The study also concluded that there were more efficient uses of the land than growing sugar cane, such as coffee and cash food crops. This largely reflects the less than ideal climate, soils and pests for growing sugar cane in PNG (the climate is essentially too tropical to obtain the highest sugar yields) and milling throughput of about half that needed to achieve economies of scale. According to RSL, its production costs per tonne of sugar is in the middle range mainly due to the factory's small size.

Source: Fleming and Hardaker (1997).

PNG's tariff reforms need to be implemented without further slippage ...

There has already been a delay in the introduction of the PNG tariff reform program, such that reductions are being phased in over six years to 2006, instead of the eight-years as originally intended. This is still slightly longer than the five-year program announced in 1995 but, given the very real strains of adjustment, little extra would be achieved from accelerating the program now. Instead, it would be better to focus on ensuring that the current program is fully implemented without further slippage. This in itself will be a substantial political challenge, given past experiences. Many of the substantive tariff reductions on sensitive products have been backloaded in the program. Pressures are likely therefore to intensify later for the government to delay certain tariff reductions on sensitive items. Policy makers should be ready and well equipped to refute these pressures when they arise. There will also be the question of continuing with further tariff reductions after 2006.

... rather than further delaying the reforms

Those enjoying protection currently can be expected to argue that the certain costs of adjustment may exceed the uncertain benefits from trade liberalization. They and others will also ask: Where would the new jobs come from? Two points need to be remembered on the first issue. First, economic growth abroad as well as at home imposes adjustment costs on society all the time, and will increasingly as globalization proceeds. Empirical evidence from a myriad of studies show that the adjustments stimulated by policy reform typically are very small compared with those from all the other adjustment pressures. And second, the adjustment costs need be paid only once, whereas the benefits from resources being relocated in activities that are more competitive internationally flow on forever. Similarly, arguments to delay trade and investment liberalization until other policies, such as institutional and governance weaknesses, are reformed are not convincing.

Where, though, will the new jobs come from?

Even though more could have been produced and perhaps more jobs created by other industries had protection not been introduced, wouldn't it be better to leave workers in those protected jobs now that they are established? It is difficult for anyone, including governments, to say precisely where new jobs would come from following comprehensive trade reforms, because too many things change simultaneously. Nonetheless, the experiences of many countries over the past two decades suggest there is every reason to be optimistic — especially if good macroeconomic policy is practiced during and beyond the adjustment period (Corden 1997).

PNG's taxation review includes tariffs

The PNG Government has commissioned a full review of its tax system, due to be completed by 30 September 2000. The Taxation Review (headed by Sir Nagora Bogan) is intended to provide the Government with recommendations on all aspects of tax policy formulation and implementation, including tariff arrangements. It is to review the process by which general import tariffs are set, the duty drawback scheme and related procedures, as well as dumping arrangements. PNG's WTO commitments are relevant to this review.

Other economic reforms

Across-the-board tariff cuts for PNG

PNG's tariff reform program is reasonably comprehensive and applies across-the-board tariff reductions. However, as indicated above, tariffs on a small range of sensitive products have received special treatment by being allowed to remain high until late into the six-year program. Moreover, tariffs on some products were increased under the program, namely from 11% to either 30% or 40% on a range of foodstuffs.

Reform should cover both input and output markets

Reforming output markets alone is insufficient, and may even worsen resource use efficiency and compound the short-term adjustment costs of reform. Efficient firms will have difficulty competing with imports under lower tariffs if they remain subject to inefficient input prices. This includes not only raw materials but also other inputs such as labour and government-supplied infrastructure services.

High tariffs on inputs penalize efficiency

For PNG, this means that decisions to slow down the tariff reductions on important raw material inputs, such as sugar and cement, will continue to penalize more efficient industries. Consequently, those already lowly assisted industries undergoing faster reductions in tariffs on their outputs relative to inputs would have been made worse off to date by the reform program. This limits the scope for newly efficient industries, including exporters, to expand.

Efficiently provided services are fundamental for growth ...

As well, there is an urgent need in PNG to reform the government-provision of essential business inputs, such as transport, telecommunications and electricity. These continue to be provided by state-owned monopolies at internationally high prices and sub-standard quality. Coastal shipping, for example, is protected by government cabotage policies that prevent foreign shippers from competing on domestic routes. While this protects the incumbent firm, it has made coastal shipping, an essential service input used widely in PNG, very expensive. It is important therefore that this market, along with other service inputs, be deregulated to better enable PNG industry to compete internationally. PNG and other small island economies are inherently high-cost economies because of their size and distance from major markets, so it is imperative that these costs be kept to a minimum if a thriving and diversified export base is to be achieved. PNG's Government is committed to privatize some of its state-owned enterprises, which is an important beginning. But replacing a public monopoly with a private one need not, on its own, be a great improvement. What is also essential is to ensure that the markets those enterprises operate in are made contestible. One way for a small country to help that happen is to allow liberal access to foreign investment.

... including law and order ...

Deterioration in other public services, especially the law and order problem, must also be corrected. The immense law and order problem not only affects the quality of life of

PNG residents, but also directly inflates business costs and thereby contributes substantially to PNG's high-cost economy. It remains the single biggest impediment to business in PNG (Duncan and Lawson 1997). It was estimated that direct security costs of firms amounted to 3% of total production costs and that the indirect costs of crime may be as high as 9% of costs. In GDP terms, these represent about 0.8% and 1.3% of GDP (Levantis 1997).

... and realistic labour costs

Labour costs are fundamental to the international competitiveness of PNG industry. Under the regulated labour market system inherited from Australia at independence, real labour costs (adjusted for productivity levels) increased to uneconomic levels. Since the deregulation of the labour market in 1992 by the Minimum Wages Board, such costs have declined. This has resulted in a large increase in employment. The 1992 labour market reforms were apparently successful in stimulating some private sector employment, which grew by 17% between 1993 and 1998 (Levantis 2000). This compares favourably with almost stagnant employment growth in the two decades following independence. However, the private sector is only a small part of the total PNG workforce and is incapable of absorbing the large number of school leavers each year. Hence, that employment growth figure is not inconsistent with the deteriorating law and order situation and the country's increased macroeconomic instability.

Recent wage developments raise concern

The PNG Government decided to re-establish the Minimum Wages Board and following the latest round of hearings, has offered to raise the minimum wage by more than Kina 5 per week. While this may seem a small rise, and is well below the exorbitant claims of some unions, it is only affordable if it is matched by increased productivity levels. If this also re-introduces rigidities into the labour market, it could contribute to unemployment and impose additional adjustment costs on the economy as tariff reforms are implemented. Again this is not a reason to abort the reform process, but rather a reminder of the interconnectedness of the various markets for inputs and outputs.

Comprehensive reforms can reduce adjustment costs

The advantages of making the reform program as comprehensive as possible are not only that the potential gains from trade liberalization are increased, but as well the adjustment costs could be reduced. Gains are increased because it lessons the chance that resources will flow out of one inefficient use into another that has had its protection level preserved. The adjustment costs can be lower rather than higher with comprehensive reform because the benefits of reform are expanded, thereby providing greater capacity for the economy to absorb elsewhere the dislocated resources. It also helps minimize the problem of multiple adjustments, which could occur if a partial reform causes resources to flow from one inefficient activity to another, only to have to undergo subsequent adjustment following further reforms.

Structural adjustment is fundamental to economic growth ...

Structural adjustment is always occurring in any economy in response to changes in consumer tastes, technology, incomes and production techniques. Without it, economies would under-perform. The more flexible are an economy's productive factors to continuous change, the smoother will be the process of adjustment. While capital is reasonably mobile and can generally flow into alternative uses, labour can be less mobile between different industries, occupations and regions.

Handling the adjustment costs of reform

... even though it raises political difficulties

In any economy, whether it be relative large economies or much smaller economies like those in the Pacific, a major obstacle to governments reforming trade policies is being able to withstand the political consequences inherent in the structural adjustment pressures induced by such policy changes. Governments understandably try to minimize those political costs by announcing that policy changes will be phased in gradually. In PNG's case, the Government has introduced a six-year program of tariff reforms to give stakeholders plenty of time to respond. This also raises questions of equity and fairness: should the government provide compensation to those adversely affected by the reforms?

Large structural adjustment pressures indicate large potential economic gains from trade reforms ...

While the costs of structural adjustment induced from trade reforms impact relatively quickly and are obvious, the benefits of such reforms — while they go on forever — tend to be more diffuse throughout the community and less visible. But it must be remembered that where substantial adjustment pressures follow, so too will the potential economic benefits from such reforms be greatest. Thus, large structural adjustment pressures are the flip side of reaping potentially large economic gains from restructuring, and are thus as much a measure of the opportunity for economic prosperity as they are of the one-off adjustment cost. Put simply, it is impossible to realize significant economic benefits from policy reforms without having substantial structural adjustment: with the gain comes some pain. Thus efforts by PNG and other governments to avoid the adjustment pressures of reforms also seriously risk reducing or at least delaying the economic gains from these reforms.

... and from correcting past policy mistakes

The identification of areas of large structural adjustment needed following trade reforms is perhaps the best indicator available that policies have imposed efficiency costs on the economy and that production patterns are out of kilter with the country's comparative advantage. If government policies of providing high selective protection to certain industries had been successful, then removing such assistance would be possible with minimal restructuring. Thus, the lesson for governments should be to avoid in future being party to special deals with the private sector that provide high levels of selective assistance. Because of the implications, governments, once heavily committed in such projects, are often reluctant to admit to their mistakes and instead frequently provide more assistance in the hope that the industry will turn around and become commercially viable without government assistance in the longer run. But more often than not this does not happen, which only compounds the problems.

Policy instability compounds adjustment costs

The best means by which governments can facilitate adjustment is to phase in reforms and to preannounce them[19]. Back tracking on reforms and policy instability will increase adjustment costs. The government must be committed to the program to ensure that they are fully implemented. In PNG, this has been a major problem with past reform programs. Because the costs of reform normally come first, it is imperative that the reform program does not stall mid-term. Otherwise the society incurs the costs but does not reap the benefits. This seems to have given trade and other economic reforms a bad name in PNG, both among the community and within certain segments of government. As such, there appears to be, in some circles at least, a general reluctance to embrace change as a source of economic prosperity. Reversing community attitudes on reform is a slow and difficult process, and requires the government to actively inform the community of precisely what reforms are to be introduced and when, and then to stick to that program. Policy reforms must be both clear and credible for the private sector to be able to plan ahead with confidence.

Is there a role for structural adjustment assistance?

Can the provision of adjustment assistance help? In the Ramu sugar case, for example, should the government provide financial assistance to workers and the community adversely affected by the reforms if Ramu sugar closes or contracts its operations following reduced government assistance? Help could come in the form of worker re-location assistance or re-training for displaced workers. What appears to make Ramu sugar special is the potential magnitude of the adjustment involved. It employs some 1,500 workers in the Ramu valley, and a community of several more thousand people currently depend on Ramu sugar for income. This would appear the strongest case in PNG for adjustment assistance, but any such scheme

---

[19] However, even this is not costless to the community since it involves also delaying the realization of benefits by the community from reform.

would need to be carefully designed to avoid the pitfalls often associated with them. More often then not, specific adjustment schemes are based not so much on economic considerations, but are seen as a way of easing the short-term adjustment pressures and therefore making the reforms more palatable for the community and governments. In this context, such schemes may play a useful role, but they need to be tightly scrutinized and applied only in extreme cases where policy changes are not possible otherwise[20].

Implement-ation problems of such schemes makes them of dubious value

The provision of structural adjustment assistance involves many practical problems that, if not handled properly, may work against reform and give it a bad name. First, it requires policymakers to be able to identify who needs compensation and what the correct level should be. There are also moral hazard problems. Just as selective assistance bestows benefits to some industries while imposing adjustment costs on other, lowly assisted industries, so selective adjustment assistance is also discriminatory, in favour of those that receive it. That is, the schemes themselves can introduce inequities in addition to inefficiencies. Furthermore, if not well designed such schemes in practice can provide an incentive not to adjust[21]. Despite their intentions, structural adjustment

---

[20] In the case of the recent reform of the Australian dairy market, for example, the government introduced a payment scheme for farmers. This maintains the domestic consumer price of milk above the international price during the adjustment period, but the difference is collected as a tax to fund a one-off grant to producers to assist them become more efficient (e.g. by getting bigger) or to move to another activity. For details of that Dairy Industry Adjustment Program, see www.affa.gov.au/diap

[21] This stems largely from the political economy driving such schemes. Governments are nearly always compelled to direct the assistance to factors that are not coping with the adjustment, rather than rewarding those that adjust successfully. For example, worker re-training schemes assist those that have not been able to adjust on their own accord, while workers that have successfully adjusted receive no assistance, even though they may have incurred substantial costs in re-training and gaining alternative employment.

schemes can thereby end up hindering rather than facilitating adjustment and fair outcomes.

... even if there is no general safety net for workers

It is generally argued that structural adjustment is best handled by economies having a general safety net, such as welfare payments, to ease the labour adjustment problems. These are preferred over adopting special schemes for individual industries. However, PNG does not have a general welfare system. Even so, it is difficult to argue that workers displaced because of a subset of policy-induced reforms should receive assistance that is not available to other workers who also incur structural dislocation due to other policy reforms or indeed general (non-policy-induced) economic changes.

Possible role for donors

Providing funds to pay for adjustment schemes to facilitate industry restructuring may be a possible role for major donor assistance. However, such schemes would need to be tightly controlled to ensure that the intended restructuring occurred.

The most effective role for the PNG Government

Are adjustment costs of reform more than the benefits?

International empirical studies suggest that, although significant in a few situations, the adjustment costs of trade liberalization are generally small in relation to the benefits, usually as little as one-twentieth (Matusz and Tarr 1999). The most effective role for the PNG government is to focus on the fundamental problems contributing to high and prolonged adjustment costs, and find ways to minimize them.

Supportive institutional arrangements are needed to facilitate adjustment

Without supportive institutional arrangements, adjustment costs will be increased and the private sector will be incapable of providing the necessary impetus needed to provide efficient and longer term growth. Also, governments should remove impediments to adjustment, such as labour market rigidities, investment restrictions and inappropriate and unstable macroeconomic polices, while ensuring that structural reforms are appropriately sequenced. These factors will facilitate the quickest and sustained response in newly emerging competitive sectors of the economy.

Maintaining a competitive rate for the kina will also help

Economic performance and adjustment to economic changes is closely linked to the flexibility of the kina's exchange rate. There is little doubt that had PNG maintained its 'hard kina' policy the adjustment costs of trade liberalization would have been much greater. Introducing a flexible exchange rate in 1994 enabled the over-valued kina to fall, thereby benefiting exporters through enhanced export returns and improving the international competitiveness of PNG's import-competing industries by raising import parity prices. From 1994 to 1998, the kina devalued by around 40% in nominal terms and 22% in real terms (the difference being due to PNG's higher inflation rate compared to that of major trading partners). The benefits to the PNG economy, including to the agricultural sector, of maintaining a competitive exchange rate have been demonstrated in several studies (Box 4.5).

Trade reforms are easier with a flexible exchange rate

Thus, substantial currency devaluations since 1994 have supplemented the effects of tariffs and boosted PNG's international competitiveness against imports. This has provided a lower-cost opportunity to reduce tariffs substantially. Those industries that have retained much higher tariffs until 2006, however, have effectively had their 'protection' against imports increased, especially when the large kina devaluation also is taken into account. Moreover, as tariffs are lowered under the reform program, further currency deprecations provide one means of partly offsetting the adverse effects of tariff reductions on PNG industry. The government should therefore avoid intervening in the foreign exchange market as it did in 1999, should the kina depreciate during the remainder of the tariff reform program, for to do so may compound the adjustment costs and threaten the reform program itself.

Box 4.5: Modeling the Supply Response of Devaluation of the Kina

This box discussed four reputable studies that have shown substantial benefits to the PNG economy following the adoption of a more flexible exchange rate. These are:

Study One (Woldekidan 1994)

This modeled the short-run impact of a 10% devaluation of the kina under the assumptions of wage flexibility and restrictive monetary policy. The key findings were:

-real GDP would increase by 2.5%;

-real exports would increase by 5.9% and imports decrease by 5.6%; and

-smallholder coffee output would increase by 7%, and smallholder palm oil by45%.

Study Two (World Bank 1996)

This study concluded that a 20% kina devaluation would increase average rural income by 7% and that of poor rural households by 13-17%, due to export expansion and import substitution.

Box 4.5: Modeling the Supply Response of Devaluation of the Kina (continued)

Study Three (Fallon, King and Zeitsch 1995)

This modeled the short-run impact of a 20% kina devaluation while holding output in the smallholder sector constant and making 'elasticity pessimistic' assumptions. It concluded that:

-real GDP would increase by 1.6%;

-real exports would increase by 1.9% and imports decline by 2.7%; and

-forestry output would increase by 12.7%.

Study Four (Duncan et al 1998)

The study concluded that the output for key tree crops was responsive to prices and changes in the real kina exchange rate, including:

- a 10% real depreciation is associated with a 24% expansion in coffee production and a 34% increase in copra;

- the responsiveness of coffee and copra production to the exchange rate was indicative of significant under-utilisation of productive potential and a high level of pass-through of higher export prices to farmers (due to a competitive marketing chain for coffee); and

- in contrast, cocoa production was found to be relatively unresponsive to changes in the real kina exchange rate because the heavily regulated marketing chain reduced the level of pass-through of higher export prices to farmers.

- *Source:* AusAID (1999).

Governments must know their vital role and do only what they can do best

The PNG Government has a vital role in providing good governance and a sound economic and political environment to ensure privately profitable business activities and investments are also socially profitable. This includes providing fundamental institutions and laws discussed elsewhere in this report, such as enforceable property rights, a well-functioning legal system and bankruptcy laws that protect creditors – actions that are all needed for a market economy to function efficiently. Underpinning this is the need for sound and stable macroeconomic policies.

Six basic principles of good government:

Thus, adopting market-friendly policies does not necessarily mean less government involvement. Rather it means governments should limit their interventions to ensuring the provision of essential public goods and offsetting the most problematic market failures and externalities. More specifically, the Government should:

- take a vital, but often indirect, role in establishing beneficial institutions and necessary infrastructure;

- create competitive conditions by making markets contestable (the credible threat of new entrants may be enough to ensure the incumbents behave competitively);

- adopt productivity-enhancing policies, such as quality education, health and sound infrastructure, including in rural areas, and by pro-competitive microeconomic policy reforms;

- ensure that property rights, including over natural resources such as timber, fish and minerals, are well established and enforced, as well as such returns being appropriatly taxed, for example, via measures such as resource rent taxes and stumpage fees designed to ensure sustainable management[22];

---

[22] Some reports suggest, for example, that PNG and the Solomon Islands governments have under-priced fishing and timber resources, and that the issuance of licences have been associated with corrupt

- achieve political and economic stability; and

- ensure that the exchange rate truly reflects the nation's economic fundamentals by letting it find its own level.

Areas of future growth

Predicting growth areas before reforms are allowed to work is difficult ...

Predicting which specific productive activities will succeed following reforms is virtually impossible. New activities must evolve from the interaction of many markets. It is also often not clear what the effects of trade and investment liberalization will be on existing protected industries. While those that cannot compete with imports will contract and may close completely, some will certainly survive and may even prosper through rationalizing their operations, becoming more competitive, and possibly acquiring those that would otherwise close.

... but the primary sector clearly will be a major beneficiary of the reforms

The primary sector will continue for the foreseeable future to hold a key to the future economic development of PNG. Better (i.e. sustainable) economic exploitation of its agricultural and natural resource-based industries, of timber, minerals and fish, are fundamental to the economy's success. However, this does not necessarily mean that these primary products should be fully processed by PNG. Resource-rich economies, such as PNG and the Solomon Islands, are often better off exporting raw or semi-processed materials for processing overseas[23]. Processing, like any activity, must be efficient if it is to add to national welfare (see Appendix 4).

Agriculture is vital for many reasons ...

Since 85% of PNG's people live in rural areas and agriculture is important in production and exports, it is central not only to national economic growth but also to poverty alleviation. The reforms suggested in this report will help to remove the disincentives currently facing

---

practices. Administrative arrangements need to be transparent and free from political interference to reduce the risk of such practices.

[23] This is not unusual. Successful primary-based economies all tend to export far greater quantities of unprocessed commodities for overseas processing than are processed at home.

farmers to invest in improving the quality of their farm land and to efficiently produce tree crops like cocoa, coffee, copra, cocoa and palm oil (Box 4.6). The government can play a key role by ensuring that there is sufficient funding for agricultural research and development and for the dissemination of R&D findings (Jarrett and Anderson 1989). Equally, the government can inhibit growth by using protective industrialization measures such as those aimed at generating a domestic fishing industry or log processing, as practiced in PNG and other Pacific island economies (Box 4.7).

Box 4.6: Agricultural Production in PNG

Studies on PNG agriculture have consistently found that:

-it is a high-cost producer of most of its agricultural products due to high labour, transportation, marketing and management costs as well as overheads;

-smallholders are relatively more efficient than largeholders at producing export crops; and

-palm oil production appears to be the most internationally competitive, although even that is difficult to judge as the government has been a joint venturer.

Some other crops have had their competitiveness improved since the mid-1990s following the kina devaluations. However, commercial production of eggs, poultry, sugar, cereals, including rice, pork, and to a lesser extent beef remain non-competitive. Livestock industries have in the past been penalized by the high tariffs on imported feed designed to assist the domestic animal feed industry.

Source: WTO (1999).

... as is mineral development... The PNG economy is already heavily dependent on oil and minerals. The potential for further developing this sector is substantial provided PNG provides an 'enabling' and stable environment to attract foreign investment and allow such large projects to develop profitably. For example, the propo-sal to construct a world-scale liguified natural gas (LNG) manufacturing plant in 2003-05 to develop the Hides gas field and export gas at premium prices to rapidly developing countries like Korea and China would enormously benefit the PNG economy.

It would create some 27,000 jobs (a 10% increase), raise national income by as much as 10%, and boost, by as much as 25%, government revenue (Box 4.8). However, the feasibility of such a project relies heavily on the government adopting more market-friendly policies as well as improving economic governance and the basic infrastructure needed to facilitate private sector development. Such policies will also reduce the 'enclave' nature of the mining sector by encouraging foreign firms to have a greater presence in PNG, thereby contributing to the beneficial 'flow-on' effects from mining to the rest of the economy.

Other petroleum projects are also under consideration which would also boost PNG development. The construction of a pipeline to supply gas to Queensland from the Kutuba and Pandora fields, is planned to commence by 2002, following a Memorandum of Understanding signed with the Queensland Government.

... and services Services already account for 40% of GDP in PNG. Some service industries could expand if reforms were put into place. Tourism is a good example, given PNG's natural beauty, but it has stagnated because of the law and order problem and inadequate infrastructure. Between 1970 and 1993, the average annual growth in tourism was -1%. It has been estimated that expenditure by international tourists equivalent to 15% of PNG's GDP could be generated if these problems were overcome (Duncan and Lawson 1997).

Box 4.7: Economic Pitfalls of Using Trade Barriers to Achieve Resource and Environmental Objectives and Promote Domestic Processing

It has been common practice in PNG and other Pacific island economies for governments to intervene using trade barriers to promote processing and industrialization. A variety of trade barriers are used for this purpose. The most common is to maintain an escalating tariff structure that provides higher tariff protection for more processed products. Despite some recent improvements, PNG and the Solomon Islands maintain an escalating tariff structure that is designed to encourage value added by providing very high effective rates of protection (ERP) to downstream processing. Coffee processing, for example, attracted an ERP of 30% in the early 1990s while food processing had ERPs ranging from 106% to 228% (Table 4.1).

Other trade barriers used to promote domestic processing of raw materials are export taxes and prohibitions, and domestication policies that promote increased domestic participation in the industry through investment and licensing controls. PNG and the Solomon Islands, for example, maintain export taxes on unprocessed logs and intend to prohibit log exports. Similarly, the principal objective of fishery policy in these and most other island economies is to 'domesticate' the industry through discriminatory investment and licensing policies aimed at encouraging local fishing fleets and downstream processing. PNG and other members of the Forum Fisheries Agency ban high seas transshipment and impose mandatory requirements on them to use designated ports and use of domestic facilities. Moreover, domestic fishing fleets receive preferential access to fishing licenses.

However, such domestication policies may raise efficiency concerns if such activity is not economically viable. Imposing mandatory port requirements on foreign fishing fleets is effectively placing local content plans on them requiring them to source a share of their inputs domestically in return for access to fishing rights.

Box 4.7: Economic Pitfalls of Using Trade Barriers to Achieve Resource and Environmental Objectives and Promote Domestic Processing (continued)

Current policies in PNG favour the high risk option of potentially larger but highly uncertain gains from 'domestication' of the tuna industry (which may be inefficient) over smaller but more certain benefits from collecting access license fees from foreign vessels. Imposing mandatory requirements on foreign operators that raise their costs risks inefficiently dissipating the rent premium paid on fishing licenses. If this happens, island economies could end up receiving lower access fees from foreign vessels.

Similarly, the efficacy of using export taxes or prohibitions on round logs promote processing is questionable on economic grounds. Taxing or prohibiting exports of unprocessed logs assists downstream processing by diverting export sales on to the home market. The domestic price is thus reduced by the export restriction, providing an implicit subsidy to processors and penalizing raw material suppliers. Domestic prices would be expected to fall by the full amount of the export tax, or where the taxes are prohibitive or export of the logs banned, by a potentially larger amount. Because export restrictions lower input prices, they can provide substantial effective rates of assistance to value added by downstream processors. This is particular the case for processed wood products that also receive a high level of tariff protection. Indeed, if the implicit input subsidy and tariffs become large enough, the downstream processed activity may subtract, rather than add, value. Such inefficient processing would be economically undesirable and would risk frittering away the economy's natural resources without any lasting benefit to the country. This is particularly the case for plywood and other laminated boards in PNG, which continue to be subject to high tariffs of currently 95% (down from 100%) while also benefiting from the export restriction on logs. This is not to argue against sound environmental policies for fishing or logging, but rather to argue for the use of more-efficient measures to achieve those (and perhaps tax revenue-raising) objectives.

Source: WTO (1999).

Box 4.8: Mineral Development in PNG

The LNG project proposed by the BP-Esso-Oil Search consortium would be the biggest resource development project ever undertaken in PNG. It involves K3.3 billion being spent on a gas field at Hides, pipelines to Kutubu and Wewak, a central processing facility at Tagari, and a large LNG plant and wharf at Wewak. It would have far-reaching direct and indirect benefits on the PNG economy, raising national income by some 5-10%. Jobs would be increased by 25% and additional exports generated of up to K1.7 billion.

However, PNG's economic policies must be sufficiently flexible to enable such development since such a large resource project is likely to reduce or 'crowd out' the growth prospects of other industries, including the agriculture sector, through exchange rate effects — the so-called 'Dutch disease.' The project's development will also require the PNG Government to ensure an expansion of skilled labour and to provide the necessary roads and other infrastructure needed for the project. A vital aspect will also be the certainty with which developers are provided mining rights by the government through agreements with landowners and stability of the taxation arrangements. Appropriate environmental regulations will also need to be determined and applied with certainty.

The Dutch disease is a term coined by economists to describe a situation encountered by the Netherlands following development of new natural gas reserves in the North Sea. Development of these fields was associated with depressed performance of the manufacturing sector, and has since been found to occur in many other resource-rich countries, such as Britain, Norway, Australia, Mexico and PNG.

Box 4.8: Mineral Development in PNG (continued)

The Dutch disease stems from the exchange rate effects on the rest of the economy of large mineral exports and inflows of foreign direct investment needed to develop substantial resource projects. These inflows appreciate the country's exchange rate thereby reducing the international competitiveness of manufactured and other 'traded' goods (including agriculture), both in export markets and domestically against imports. Resources flow out of these sectors into the mineral sector and non-traded activities, such as services, and manufacturing contracts. The extent to which the mineral sector attracts labour and capital away from manufacturing by bidding up wages and interest rates will depend upon whether or not it is an 'enclave' activity.

Catching the Dutch disease is not necessarily a problem. However a relatively small industrial sector is likely to be a natural outcome of having a rich resource base. Thus, efforts to control the exchange rate or to promote industrialization through import protection are likely to be counterproductive. Resources must come from somewhere else in the economy if the mining sector is to expand as a 'non-enclave' activity. There is nothing inherently right or wrong about shifting resources from manufacturing into mining. A contracting manufacturing sector can be associated with strong growth in other sectors and should not therefore be seen as an undesirable outcome.

Source: WTO (1999) and CIE (1997).

5

How can WTO help boost Pacific Island development?

Past protectionist policies have not worked

Good governance as well as widespread economic reforms, including trade and investment liberalization, are essential to PNG's and the region's long term economic prosperity. Past policies, based on selective protection and state intervention, have clearly not worked in terms of generating economic growth and sustainable development. To what extent can compliance with WTO commitments benefit PNG and other Pacific island governments to perform better, and what political costs are involved? Answering that question requires assessing the extent to which WTO membership can make it easier for governments to deliver domestic reforms.

The WTO membership queue is a good sign of its worth

The fact that almost 140 countries are WTO members, and that the number is increasing rapidly with 30 developing and transition economies currently in the queue to join, are clear indications that most governments see it in their own interests to join the WTO.

The WTO's predecessor, the GATT, was formed in 1948 as a means of countering the spread of protectionism that threatened to sub-divide the world into trading blocs and to undermine world economic prosperity (see Appendix 3 for details). Its long-term objective is a more open global trading system based on freer trade whereby disputes are settled multilaterally.

WTO involves multilateral reforms

The WTO is based on multilateral reductions in protection. This can be contrasted with APEC, for example, which relies on members unilaterally lowering protection in a co-ordinated but voluntary framework (see Chapter 6).

Approaches to reform

Two options: unilateral or multilateral reductions

There are two possible approaches available to PNG and all governments to reforming trade and protection policies. They can introduce such policies unilaterally, in other words, on their own accord irrespective of external developments. Alternatively, they can negotiate such reductions multilaterally within the WTO by undertaking binding commitments not to apply non-tariff measures and to progressively reduce tariff levels.

Unilateral trade reform is possible

Since trade policy is set at home by governments responding to domestic political pressures, unilateral measures are the most effective means of implementing trade reforms. Thus, the PNG government could effectively go ahead and implement trade reforms without the WTO. Indeed, this is what PNG has done recently with the current tariff reform program.

But WTO complements and strengthens unilateral efforts

Having said that, however, the WTO can provide an effective means of complementing unilateral trade reforms. WTO membership provides an additional reason for governments to apply sound economic policy making. Governments are required to make binding policy commitments, which then provide a means of resisting domestic lobbying pressures for protection. By choosing to make international commitments with the WTO, a country can 'lock in' its unilateral reforms as a means of limiting future policy backsliding. It is also often easier for governments to sell such reforms at home when they can show that similar foreign producers are also being affected, and that such reforms will benefit exporters by securing greater market access to overseas markets. This is particularly important for countries like PNG that have weak economic governance and find it difficult to implement on their own accord sustainable trade reforms.

Usefulness depends on the extent of WTO members' commitments ...

However, while members take on board a number of fundamental commitments on how to conduct trade policy when joining the WTO, several individual commitments, such as on tariff levels and services liberalization, are negotiated individually either as part of their accession or during consecutive rounds of multilateral trade negotiations. Thus, the effectiveness of a member's WTO commitments in promoting domestic reform will also depend on the strength of its obligations. Modest commitments on tariffs, for example, may appear to be a good negotiated outcome for a government from a domestic political viewpoint, but the downside for the economy is that it provides future governments greater scope to protect domestic industries, thereby undermining the very useful disciplinary role that that WTO membership can play.

... and the institutional setup at home

Mere membership of the WTO will not produce automatic results, however. Governments must still 'do the hard yards' at home in promoting economic reforms. The institutional setup at home, which determines the interaction between a member's government and the WTO, has an important bearing on whether such membership can be effective in promoting domestic economic reforms.

Trade departments are usually responsible for a country's WTO membership and its rights and obligations. However, they themselves can become an obstacle to trade reforms by supporting protectionist policies that are seen to be holding onto their power base domestically, or a means of retaining 'negotiating coin' in future multilateral rounds[24]. Setting good trade policy requires an economy-wide perspective that distances itself from narrower sectoral interests. Therefore, placing trade and sectoral

---

[24] It should be remembered that trade negotiations over tariffs are on 'bound' duty rates and not actual applied rates. (During the Uruguay Round negotiations, every government tabled a Schedule of tariff rates for each good traded, and they are then obliged not to raise the tariff on that good above the rate in their particular Schedule.) Thus, lowering applied levels need not undermine a member's tariff negotiating position; on the contrary, it may even strengthen it.

responsibilities together within one Trade and Industry ministry, as is frequently the case and as was done recently in PNG, may raise concerns that trade policy will become subservient to narrow industry interests at the expense of broader national welfare.

Benefits of WTO to PNG and other Pacific island economies

'Trading rules of the game' bring predictability to trade ...

Like all WTO members, PNG has agreed to implement its trade policies in accordance with WTO rules that have been negotiated by members. These rules amount to commitments or obligations by the membership. Thus, the WTO functions primarily as a rules-based system designed to make the global trading environment more predictable and liberal. Establishing 'trading rules of the game' facilitates international trade and helps safeguard the interests of all trading nations, whether small or large. Thus, the WTO is effectively the umpire of the multilateral trading system.

... and were strengthened by the Uruguay Round

The latest WTO agreements were negotiated during the Uruguay Round of Multilateral Trade Negotiations, concluded in 1994. These strengthened existing disciplines on the use of trade measures, including tariff reductions, and introduced new substantive disciplines in agriculture, services, textiles and intellectual property rights.

WTO can assist domestic policy reform

WTO offers a common sense approach to trade policy reform

The WTO is based on a number of fundamental general principles that are central to good trade and economic policy reform. Each WTO member is committed to ensuring that its trade policies meet these principles. In so doing, the multilateral trading system is strengthened and all members improve their own economic welfare when all adopt sound open market policies. Because individual policy reforms are being taken multilaterally by all members, the economic benefits accruing to each member from its reforms are much greater than if each country acted alone.

Individual countries gain from reforming even if others remain protectionist

However, what might seem like the reverse of the above, that individual economies do not benefit from trade reforms if other countries do not also reform, is false. In fact most of the benefit from multilateral reform comes from reducing one's own trade distortionary measures, so it follows that that large proportion of the gains will still be enjoyed if other countries do not at the same time change their policies.

Trade barriers should be non-discriminatory

Most-favoured-nation (MFN) treatment is essential for fairness

The cornerstone of the GATT/WTO is that a country's trade barriers should not discriminate between where the import is sourced. In other words, if PNG provides a lower tariff to imports from a certain country then this rate should apply to all of PNG's trading partners. Ensuring that its trade measures and tariff reforms conform to this principle is consistent with PNG achieving maximum economic benefits from trade reforms.

Trade creation improves efficiency, while trade diversion may not

The problem with discriminatory liberalization that provides lower tariffs to imports from certain sources is that such preferential treatment may distort imports by PNG away from the most efficient world supplier. If such trade diversion predominates, national welfare will be reduced. What is needed to raise national welfare is trade creation, whereby domestic production is replaced by cheaper imports, rather than simply replacing general-sourced imports with preferential imports. PNG's tariff reform program is based on most-favoured-nation (MFN) liberalization, MFN meaning that whatever tariff applies to one trading partner's exports must apply to all WTO members' exports of that or 'like' products to PNG.

MFN exceptions are permitted

The GATT does permit certain exceptions to MFN liberalization, especially for developing countries. The main one is to allow members to form among themselves discriminatory free trade areas (FTAs) or custom unions whereby members accord each other preferential market access. This permission reflects the recognition by the WTO that such arrangements may benefit members by being trade creating, or can provide the basis for future wider liberalization by participants. But to improve the likelihood of such benefits, the GATT in principle requires that such preferential arrangements among members meet certain conditions, namely, that they apply to 'substantially all trade', they provide full preferences, and that trade barriers are not raised against non-participants. While not foolproof, meeting these conditions increase the likelihood that such arrangements will be on balance trade creating. Regional FTA arrangements involving developing countries are not, however, required to meet these arrangements due to the existence of the so-called 'enabling clause' within the WTO.

Implications for regional arrangements involving PNG

PNG and other Pacific island economies are members of several such regional arrangements, including the Melanesian Spearhead Group (MSG), the South Pacific Regional Trade and Economic Cooperation Agreement (SPARTECA), and the Papua New Guinea-Australia Trade and Commercial Relations Agreement (PACTRA). As well, a free trade area is currently being negotiated between (South Pacific) Forum Island Countries. Although not technically required by the WTO for arrangements involving developing countries because of the 'enabling clause', it is wise to make the product coverage of any such arrangement as wide as possible, to increase the likelihood that members will benefit from trade creation dominating trade diversion. However, the similarity of Pacific island economies means that such arrangements between them are likely to provide only negligible benefits relative to multilateral liberalization, and may in fact make some members, such as the Solomon Islands, worse off (Box 5.1).

Box 5.1: Proposed Preferential Free-Trade Area (FTA) Among Forum Island Countries

Trade ministers recently endorsed in principle the formation of a WTO-consistent free-trade area (FTA) among PNG and other FICs. This would initially cover goods, and exclude Australia and New Zealand, although the long-term integration with CER is to be examined. A draft framework is to be negotiated based on a negative list of exemptions so that it can operate for tariffs in 2001.

The costs and benefits of establishing a preferential FTA among FICs were examined in a study commissioned by the South Pacific Forum Secretariat. Another study also looked at the impact of a larger free-trade area between FICs involving Australia and New Zealand.

The economic benefits of a preferential FTA fundamentally depend upon whether it creates trade among members or simply diverts trade. While additional unassisted exports between partners will be beneficial, the case of increased imports is ambiguous. Trade diversion occurs when a preferential FTA leads to switching imports from third countries to partners, usually less efficient producers. Trade creation occurs when increased imports from member countries replace less efficient domestic production rather than displacing imports from third countries. While both will enhance regional trade among members, only when it is trade creating will there be genuine trade liberalization and welfare gains to members. Such gains will be illusory where trade diversion predominates, and may even reduce members' welfare.

Trade theory suggests that a preferential FTA among small countries with similar economic characteristics will have small or even negative net welfare effects. The empirical study by Scollay (1998) estimated small economic gains to most Forum island countries from an FTA among FICs, Cook Islands, Kiribati, Samoa and Tuvalu being made worse off. PNG was found to receive a tiny increase in GDP of 0.03%. It concluded that modest economic gains would accrue to all FICs only if the FTA was accompanied by an overall 25% MFN tariff cut. It thus confirmed the crucial importance to PNG and other FICs of non-preferential liberalization in securing economic benefits.

Box 5.1: Proposed Preferential Free-Trade Area (FTA) Among Forum Island Countries (continued)

The inclusion of Australia and New Zealand in the FTA among FICs would increase considerably the economic benefits to all FICs: greater liberalization, and hence trade creation, would be associated with increased imports from more efficient Australian and New Zealand sources. PNG's GDP would increase by almost 1.5%, equivalent to an expected annual gain of K 78 million. Although economic gains to PNG are increased substantially with the inclusion of Australia and New Zealand, they remain less than those available to PNG from substantial MFN liberalization.

It is often claimed that a FTA among FICs could provide a first step to wider trade liberalization, and encourage greater cohesion among members. However, the evidence is ambiguous. Foroutan (1998) urges caution in believing that regional trading pacts among developing countries lead to more liberal trading regimes. His analysis suggests that a FTA is neither a necessary nor sufficient condition for an open and liberal trading regime. Moreover, since a predominantly trade diverting FTA means that some members gain only at the expense of other partners, such arrangements may in fact undermine regional relations. Thus, any FTA would need to be strongly oriented towards further multilateral liberalization, supported by a set of well defined measures.

It must also be remembered that the above studies may overstate the economic benefits from a FTA among FICs. This is because experience with negotiating FTAs demonstrates clearly that if pursued for their own sake they are likely to end up being very discriminatory, by either excluding key products, or even reducing third-party access through adopting convoluted rules-of-origin requirements or due to the differential effects of other non-tariff barriers. These results are likely to increase the chances of FTAs being trade diverting, and welfare reducing on balance.

Care is needed to ensure that any FTA among PNG and other FICs is concluded in a way that promotes overall trade openness and does not frustrate MFN liberalization. If not, then it could be questionable whether the formation of such an FTA is worth the substantial administrative costs members would have to incur to service the agreement, or indeed would be making best use of the Forum Secretariat's financial and other resources.

Source: WTO (1999).

FTA much more beneficial if it facilitates wider liberalization

Empirical studies demonstrate that discriminatory regional arrangements provide at most 'second best' benefits to a country compared to MFN liberalization, and may even make some participants worse off. This is necessarily so when the trade liberalization under a FTA is with only a subset of countries, compared with a MFN liberalization which avoids the risk of trade diversion by applying any tariff cut equally to all potential providers. Wider liberalization by all participants should therefore always be an objective of any regional arrangement. Members should be encouraged to also reduce MFN trade barriers to the rest of the world. The narrower the product coverage negotiated — that is, the larger the negative list of products covered— the less the benefits (since the chances of the agreement being predominantly trade diverting are thereby increased). Negotiated outcomes from such arrangements are often narrower than intended. For example, there is evidence that the MSG Agreement involving PNG has generated few gains to members and is predominantly trade diverting, leading to the possibility of economic losses (Box 5.2).

However, evidence suggests that often FTAs are trade diverting

Regional free trade areas among developing countries have not been associated with more-liberal trading regimes, and they constitute neither a necessary nor a sufficient condition for an open and liberal trade regime (Foroutan 1998). If pursued for their own sake, such arrangements can end up excluding key (i.e., highly protected sensitive) products and be trade diversionary. Only where there has been a prior commitment to more liberal trade has such arrangements expanded trade. Thus, PNG and other members should not see the creation of regional free trade areas as an alternative to multilateral liberalization. Instead, it would be more appropriate to think of them as but a stepping stone to achieving that broader liberalization. The APEC model of 'open regionalism' could avoid these pitfalls, and provides a preferred means of encouraging regional trade (see Chapter 6).

Box 5.2: The MSG Trade Agreement

A recent study has estimated that the Melanesian Spearhead Group (MSG) Trade Agreement has been primarily trade diverting (Economic Insights 1999). Trade diversion has occurred in all main products traded under the MSG, namely fresh, chilled, and frozen beef; pasta and noodles; and cement. The only product experiencing trade creation was found to be coffee, while for canned meat and fish there was a mix of trade diversion and trade creation. This is because governments have negotiated the agreement to avoid providing tariff reductions on goods produced locally that may be threatened by concessional imports.

On this basis, it was concluded that the Agreement has had a small impact on MSG economies, most likely reducing their combined GDP by 0.03%. The upper range was an increase in GDP of 0.02%.

It is likely that Vanuatu and possibly Papua New Guinea would have gained most from the agreement at the expense of the Solomon Islands. The Solomon Islands is estimated to have borne a high share of the costs imposed by trade diversion. Papua New Guinea and Vanuatu on the other hand are estimated to have gained from an expansion in exports. These benefits are estimated to have outweighed the cost to these economies of trade diversion on other commodities.

Source: WTO (1999).

Trade restrictions should operate at the border

'National treatment' of imports avoids wasteful discrimination

Another cornerstone of the GATT is that trade barriers should operate at the border, such that internal regulations, taxes and quantitative measures should not favour domestic producers over importers. It is in the economic interests not only of its trading partners but also of the WTO member itself that domestic internal measures do not discriminate against imports by favouring domestic products. Otherwise, such measures, often non-transparent, will become disguised forms of protection. It is important that PNG remove such impediments to imports and ensure that reductions in border protection are not compensated for or frustrated by discriminatory measures operating internally. Such measures are against the GATT's Article III on national treatment obligations.

Domestic commodity taxes should apply equally to imports

This has the desired effect of preventing domestic taxes from also having a protective element. If domestic commodity taxes, such as sales, excise and value added taxes, are applied at a higher rate to imported than domestic goods, then the extent of this difference amounts to an additional tariff. Just as tariffs are an economically inefficient means of raising government revenue, so too are discriminatory commodity taxes an inefficient means of delivering protection.

PNG's tax/tariff package reflects WTO principles

PNG's program of funding its tariff reform program by introducing a 10% VAT and extending the coverage of excise duties to replace tariffs on so-called luxury items, such as up to 110% on motor vehicles which are now free of tariff, is consistent with these principles. Taxes, including VAT and excise duties, are used to raise revenue and therefore have been applied equally to domestic and imported goods. Tariffs are used to protect industries and these have been retained where such protection was deemed warranted by the Government. While both tariffs and domestic taxes raise domestic and imported prices, tariffs discriminate against imports, thereby assisting home producers by enabling domestic sales at a higher price. For taxes, the additional price on both imports and the domestic product accrue to the government as revenue. The reformed tax structure should therefore enhance PNG's economic efficiency.

However taxing inputs, such as via excise duties, can be inefficient

High excise taxes on inputs, especially fuels, can however be detrimental to the economy. For example, PNG recently increased excise duties on petrol, as a means of recouping revenue from road users for road repair. While this makes economic sense provided the tax rate correctly reflects these costs, fuels are a substantial input as well into off-road uses. For example, village fishermen that use small 'banana boats' to catch fresh fish for sale in local markets, such as in Lae, use petrol as an input but receive no excise relief. Thus, for these operations, the excise duties tax production and impose an additional cost impost on these activities. That cost impost is likely to be shared between fishermen and fish consumers in paying higher prices. The success of the Samoan alia fishery, which is also based on small boats, provides an example of how important such small fishing industries can be for island development (Box 5.3). Moreover, the payment of excise duties on fuels by other off-road users, such as for commercial fishing, farming, mining and industrial purposes, is also taxing these activities.

Even taxes on luxury items can create distortions

Similarly, the extension of excise taxes in PNG to luxury goods may also tax producers that use these goods as inputs. While for most goods this is not a problem since they are clearly consumer and not producer goods, a few goods can be both. The main example is motor cars. They are also an important input into many services and other productive activities. Since such users are not entitled to any relief of excise duties, high excise taxes on new and reconditioned cars are a substantial penalty on these activities. Moreover, although the tax does not apply to used cars, raising the price of new cars will also increase used-car prices, such that producers using cars as an input cannot escape the penalty by purchasing second-hand vehicles[25].

Box 5.3: The Samoan Alia Fishing Industry

One promising development in the pacific islands is the emergence of the Samoan alia fishery. Its growth demonstrates that fishing industries can develop with little or no support provided markets can be found. This industry is based on small vessels using long lines that operate daily from Apia. Initially, the industry targeted catching yellowfin and bigeye tuna for the Japanese and US sashimi markets, but for about five years has concentrated on albacore tuna to supply the Pago Pago cannery in American Samoa. Tuna is sold to marketers who blast freeze the tuna and ship it to the cannery in freezer containers. The size of the fleet is approaching 200 vessels, employing an estimated crew of 700, with an estimated annual catch of over 2,000 tonnes.

However, as much as 20per cent of the catch delivered to the cannery is rejected due to poor quality. The reasons for this high rejection rate need to be investigated. Another major concern is the safety of fishermen. Most boats carry only rudimentary safety equipment and many of the crew are untrained in deep-sea fishing.

Source: Duncan, Cuthbertson and Bosworth (1999).

---

[25] If such 'luxury' taxes are needed for the government to be seen to be getting tax revenue from wealthy households, perhaps exemptions for legitimate business users could be introduced.

Tariffs should be preferred to quantitative import restrictions

Tariffs are the exeption to 'national treatment'

Fundamental to the GATT is that if members insist on retaining import barriers, they should rely on tariffs rather than non-tariff measures to deliver that import protection. Thus, the GATT in principle proscribes against the use of quantitative trade restrictions and other measures restricting imports but allows countries to use tariffs as a legitimate exception to national treatment. Thus, PNG and other members are not prevented by the WTO from providing protection, but rather its rules aim at limiting such protection to tariff measures, since they are more transparent than quantitative trade barriers.

Quantitative import restrictions are prohibited

The GATT prohibits the use of quantitative import and export restrictions such as quotas on trade volumes, including bans (subject to certain exceptions). Where they do apply as exceptions, members are required to administer them in a transparent and non-discriminatory manner.

Non-tariff measures on agricultural goods have been tarrified

One of the key aspects of re-incorporating agriculture into the multilateral system by the negotiation of the Agreement on Agriculture during the Uruguay Round was to prohibit the use of non-tariff measures, including import quotas, variable import levies and discretionary import licensing. Such measures have since been converted to tariffs (the process being called tarrification). This reflects a recognition that non-tariff measures dominated agriculture protection and that there would be major advantages to the trading system and to individual members from replacing such non-transparent measures with tariffs. Members agreed to bind these rates and to reduce them on an unweighted basis over the implementation period, by an average of 36% for developed countries by 2000 and by 24% for developing countries by 2004.

Use of 'grey area' measures are prohibited

The Uruguay Round also prohibited the use of so-called 'grey area' measures, such as voluntary export restraints agreed to by exporting countries at the behest of governments of importing countries. Again, this was motivated by the desire to remove these non-transparent and highly distorting and discriminatory measures.

PNG and other Pacific island economies mainly rely on tariffs

PNG and other Pacific island economies use tariffs as the main instrument of protection. PNG had already effectively tariffied non-tariff measures by the mid-1990s. Many of the higher areas of protection in PNG were initially provided in the form of import bans and other quantitative restrictions, but these were replaced by tariffs. In so far as PNG and other island economies wish to continue to rely on tariffs to protect industries, these should be lowered and, as much as is politically possible, made more uniform in order to improve economic efficiency.

Tariff levels are bound and progressively reduced by negotiation

The GATT provides for members to bind by negotiation their tariffs on a line-by-line basis. By binding tariff rates, members commit to limiting tariff rates in future to a maximum rate set by the bound level. This rate can vary between tariff lines and applies to those lines nominated by the member. Most members, including PNG, have adopted 'ceiling' bindings on many products whereby the bound rate was above the existing rate. Over time, members agree to increase the product coverage of the bindings and to reduce bound levels. During the Uruguay Round, the coverage of tariff bindings was increased considerably and members agreed to reduce average bound tariffs substantially.

Tariff bindings increase certainty and help limit backsliding ...

Since tariffs cannot be increased above bound rates (except by negotiating compensation for affected trading partners), by binding its tariffs PNG has increased certainty for traders and investors. However, the effectiveness of bindings at limiting policy backsliding depends upon the gap between existing applied rates and bound rates.

... but there is some downside risk

If a government feels compelled to backslide, the existence of bindings may force it to resort to other measures, and those other measures may be even more distorting than those disallowed under WTO rules. However, this is not an argument for not binding or for binding at well above existing tariff levels, since such circumstances will rarely occur. A maximum gap of 10% between applied and bound levels should offer governments plenty of scope to increase tariffs in future should the political need arise.

PNG has made substantial tariff bindings and reduction commitments, to be met by the current tariff reduction program

PNG bound its entire tariff schedule during the Uruguay Round, mainly at ceiling rates of 45% for agricultural products and 40% for manufactured products. Some rates were bound at higher levels of mainly 55%, 75% and 100% for products such as sugar and certain vegetable oils. The existing tariff reform program and the reductions envisaged to a maximum rate of 40% by 2006 will satisfy its WTO commitments, although during the reform program tariffs on a few products will be above the bound level (WTO 1999). The Government of PNG should ensure in future that bound levels with the WTO are reduced in line with applied existing tariffs, and that no applied tariff exceeds its bindings.

The Solomon Islands also has bound its tariffs ...

The Solomon Islands bound its entire tariff at ceiling rates well above existing levels, of up to 150%, but mainly at 80%. Unlike PNG, the generally large gap between bound and actual levels in the Solomon Islands means that implementation of the negotiated reductions in bound tariffs is likely to have little direct effect on lowering applied tariffs. Thus, its commitments place less of a discipline on future tariff levels than do those for PNG.

... and so too has Fiji

Fiji bound most of its agricultural tariffs, but only about two-fifths of its non-agricultural tariff lines. Most items bound were at a ceiling rate of 40%, which is generally well above applied rates.

Application of national treatment is reinforced by TRIMS Agreement

The Agreement on Trade-Related Investment Measures (TRIMs) confirmed that local-content and similar provisions violated national treatment and that arrangements limiting imports to the level of exports are inconsistent with GATT provisions prohibiting quantitative restrictions. Once again, these are outlawed and should be avoided by PNG and other Pacific island economies because such policies protect domestic industries and therefore distort resource-use efficiency.

Contingent protection should be used sparingly

Contingent protection provisions exist in the WTO ...

The GATT does allow numerous so-called 'escape clauses' or contingency provisions to enable members to increase tariffs above their bound levels in certain limited circumstances. However, because excessive use or abuse of these provisions would undermine the world trading system and provide little discipline on members using trade measures to protect domestic industries, efforts have been made to constrain their use by placing on them certain conditions. The Uruguay Round introduced tighter conditions and procedures on the use of these arrangements. Nevertheless, it is generally agreed among trade economists that their application is still too loose and that tighter disciplines are needed to constrain their use. They were intended to allow governments to provide short-term increases in temporary protection, rather than as a loophole in the system for invoking continual protection in excess of members' commitments.

... including anti-dumping, safeguard and balance of payment provisions

Subject to the conditions and procedures specified in the respective agreements, the GATT permits PNG and other Pacific island economies to temporarily raise tariffs above their bindings, or take some other action such as to impose import quotas, where it can be established that:

- the country is experiencing temporary and severe balance of payments difficulties;

- anti-dumping action will be against so-called 'dumped' imports that are being exported at prices below their normal value at home and are causing or threatening to cause 'material' injury to local industries in the importing country; and/or

- safeguard action will be against imports that are causing or threatening to cause 'serious' injury to domestic industries.

Anti-dumping action is WTO legal

Anti-dumping action is allowed and can be applied by any member, including PNG and other Pacific island economies, provided certain conditions are met. Such action must follow an objective and transparent investigation into whether the imports are being 'dumped' and are causing or threatening 'material' injury to domestic competing industries. PNG and some other Pacific island economies do have anti-dumping provisions in their customs regulations. In the case of PNG, for example, these provisions have only been used once so far. The case involved cement, where it was held that dumping was occurring and an anti-dumping levy recommended; but the government has not yet imposed such a levy. The PNG Government has recently changed the administrative arrangements for anti-dumping and singled greater use of such provisions against dumped products (WTO 1999). In doing so, it would be in PNG's interests to change its arrangements to be fully compatible with the WTO requirements.

... but its continued use is likely to be bad economics ...

However, it should be kept in mind that using such anti-dumping action and other measures of contingent protection is optional in the WTO. While such trade remedies are available for coping with exceptional circumstances, their continued use to overcome a balance of payments problem or as an anti-dumping measure makes no economic sense. Similarly, continually using safeguard action is likely to be counterproductive for the economy concerned.

... and so should be avoided

If taking such action, the measures taken should be consistent with WTO provisions. That places some limits on their use and makes them transparent. However, since evidence suggests that the use of such arrangements are inadequately controlled by WTO disciplines, it would be in PNG's economic interests if it also took steps to ensure that such action did not undermine its liberalization efforts. Safeguard action against imports is always preferable economically to anti-dumping action, but it too can be abused and used excessively to provide protection.

Customs procedures should not restrict imports

Transaction valuation should be used if possible

A basic thrust of the GATT/WTO rules concerning customs procedures is that they should be transparent and not an additional barrier to imports. Thus, the WTO Agreement on Customs Valuation specifies that the transaction value method should be used for customs valuation, and specifies alternative valuation methods to be followed when this is infeasible. This improves the transparency of these arrangements and prohibits the use of minimum import prices as a means of protecting domestic producers. Using such 'inflated' import prices by customs to assess duty may in practice become a de facto means of effectively raising tariff protection. Governments may continue to use pre-shipment inspection services but are required to implement the Agreement on Pre-shipment Inspection Services to ensure that such services facilitate and not restrict trade. To encourage compliance, developing countries were given until 2000 (and for some provisions until 2003) to meet their customs commitments.

It's in PNG's interests to have transparent and clear customs procedures ...

PNG is implementing the customs requirements of the WTO (and it joined the World Customs Organization in 1998 too). It is clearly in the country's own interests to ensure that custom clearance operations work smoothly and do not become an additional impediment to trade. Long delays in clearing imports through customs can be a major obstacle to development. They also can be a major source of corruption. PNG currently uses six customs valuation methods, the main one being the transaction value method, which requires that the import price not be influenced by the relationship between buyer and seller. This is the export price paid by the importer adjusted in accordance with the customs legislation. The other valuation methods permitted in the legislation are "deductive", "similar", "identical", "computed" calculations, and as a last resort the "fallback" measure. Where a customs valuation is in dispute, the goods can be cleared provisionally if the importer lodges either a bank guarantee or cash deposit as security. PNG does not set any minimum import or reference prices for customs valuation. However, the fallback value method, the valuation method of last resort, applies certain set values (WTO 1999).

... as it is for the Solomon Islands and Fiji

The Solomon Islands intends to meet the requirements of the WTO Customs Valuation Agreement by 2002, and is currently using a valuation method for customs purposes consistent with the Brussels Definition of Value (WTO 1998b). It is also considering the introduction of pre-shipment inspection services. Fiji adopted the WTO's valuation methods from 1997 when it replaced the Brussels Definition of Value, but it does not use pre-shipment inspection.

Resolving trade disputes according to internationally-set rules

WTO has a much improved dispute settlement system

By agreeing internationally on the WTO's multilateral rules, such as the most-favoured-nation principle and national treatment, the GATT/WTO has established an important framework in which global trade can be facilitated and disputes resolved. Having these rules protects the interests of all WTO members, but in particular they safeguard the welfare of small and weak nations, such as PNG and other Pacific island economies, against possible trade discriminatory policy actions by large and powerful economies.

WTO limits actions by large countries that may be detrimental to smaller nations ...

Without such a rules-based multilateral system, small countries would have no option but to deal with large countries bilaterally. This would expose small countries to the possibility of one-sided outcomes against their own best interests. While a few large countries may have sufficient market power to influence their terms of trade by individually taxing imports and exports, trade theory shows that the rest of the world would be made worse off by these trade barriers. Moreover, if many countries followed this route, everybody could be made worse off.

... and also bilateral deals among large players at the expense of smaller ones

Similarly, without such rules, it would be easy for large countries to enter bilateral trade agreements with each other with total disregard for the trade interests of small nations. Powerful nations could, for example, bilaterally agree to exclude exports from smaller countries in preference to each other's exports.

WTO rules are particularly important for developing countries ...

While it is often alleged that WTO membership by developing countries facilitates 'exploitation' of them by developed economies, the opposite is the case in reality. Developing countries risk greater exploitation by remaining outside the WTO. As a WTO member, developing countries receive the protection offered by the multilateral system. Developing countries, working individually or in cohort with other members that have similar interests, can effectively influence these rules and the operations of the WTO. The Cairns Group on agriculture is a good example of how a diverse group of countries with a common trade interest, in this case the liberalization of agricultural trade, can collectively influence WTO outcomes.

... although there is scope to enhance the net benefits to DCs

True, there has been a lot of criticism recently from developing countries about the extent to which they are influencing outcomes at the WTO. Some of that criticism is well justified. However, the current situation is very much a consequence of the relatively passive role developing countries played in the Uruguay Round. Now that such a large number of them are WTO members, with more than 30 others seeking to join, their scope for influencing WTO processes is steadily growing. The World Bank, and others such as the United Kingdom's technical cooperation Minister, are pushing strongly in support of efforts to ensure that the next multilateral round is a 'development round' that gives much more weight than previous rounds to developing countries' concerns. Certainly there are economies of size in participating, which makes it difficult for tiny economies such as those in the South Pacific to do as much as larger nations (Michalopoulos 1998). But there are also ways of overcoming such constraints, including being represented as a regional grouping -- as ASEAN and the EU members tend to do.

WTO dispute settlement mechanism protects even non-contesting members

The WTO provides for an effective means of multilaterally resolving trade disputes in accordance with the internationally agreed rules. Members agree not to resolve disputes unilaterally, but rather to seek recourse through the WTO's Dispute Settlement Body and to abide by its rules and findings. The process therefore protects the interests of third countries not directly involved in the dispute. The emphasis is on resolution by negotiation and mediation but, failing this, the complaining country may take the case to a legal ruling by a panel.

DS Panel decisions are subject to appeal but are ultimately binding on members

Panel decisions, which may be appealed once to the Appellate Body, are now effectively binding on all WTO members. Prior to the Uruguay Round, the process enabled losing parties to a panel to veto the adoption of its findings by the GATT membership, thereby stopping the outcome from becoming legally binding on contracting parties. That possibility has now been removed.

Fundamental DS rights of WTO membership are available to all member countries ...

Any WTO member can access the dispute settlement (DS) mechanism to challenge any other members' trade policies. Thus, PNG could directly challenge the trade policies of the United States, for example, if it thought that the US had breached its WTO commitments. Similarly, any member of the WTO may nominate to be a co-complainant party to a dispute directly involving other members. A member may also choose as an interested by-stander to be a 'third party' to a dispute. This helps safeguard the interests of all potentially affected parties in such disputes. Although mounting such disputes may well exceed the financial and technical capacity of small states like PNG and other Pacific island economies, international institutions, including the WTO itself, are aware of that difficulty and are finding ways of improving access by all members to the dispute system[26]. Often the most effective option available for small states will be to take such action as a group, or in

---

[26] An example is the formation of the recent Advisory Centre on WTO Law by the WTO and the World Bank.

conjunction with other better-equipped members who are similarly grieved by another member's measures. Also, the resource demands of being a 'third party' to a dispute are minimal.

... with special provisions for supporting small members' participation in DS

Governments of small and poor developing economies of course have less financial capacity to mount a DS case before a WTO Panel than do those of larger economies. Even so, technical and financial assistance measures have been put in place for poorer WTO members to access legal support, and funds for those initiatives are being raised. As well, going into a case with several other similarly aggrieved members can spread the legal costs enough to make participation possible.

While it won't always work perfectly, so far the WTO's DS record is very good

This is not to say the DS procedures of the WTO are faultless. The European Union's slowness in bringing its banana import regime into conformity with its WTO commitments is a clear example of how difficult it is for the WTO membership to force a reluctant large player to promptly abide by DS rulings. But such exceptions have been very rare so far in the six years since the WTO DS system was introduced. More than that, the system is being actively used by developing country members, especially taking into account the size of their trade flows (Mavroidis, Nordstrom and Horn 1999).

Securing market access abroad

One country's WTO obligations are another country's rights

Because all WTO members must abide by the rules, the WTO ensures that each member receives equal access to each other's markets. This is enshrined in the most-favoured-nation (MFN) principle. In other words, if a member extends a lower tariff to imports from a certain source, then it must extend the same tariff to all WTO members, subject to certain exemptions.

This provides small nations greater certainty over export markets

This provides greater certainty and security for PNG and other Pacific island exporters. They know that governments of major export markets, such as the US, EU and Australia, cannot provide preferential access to competing exports from other members (again with a few exceptions such as under the EU-ACP Lome Convention and the generalized system of preferences).

Multilateral liberalization also offers improved access to foreign markets

Since the key objective of the WTO is trade liberalization, members periodically negotiate multilaterally for the removal or relaxation of trade barriers, including tariffs. This was last done in the Uruguay Round, which is to be fully implemented by 2006. By agreeing to multilateral reductions in protection, members receive, in return for opening their own markets to imports, improved access to foreign markets for their exports — the so-called principle of reciprocity, upon which the WTO and the multilateral trading system is fundamentally based. Thus, WTO members benefit from improved non-discriminatory access to export markets.

Multilateral negotiations can stimulate trade liberalization...

By exchanging market access, members can promote trade liberalization by changing the political equilibrium in trading nations. While liberalization may harm a country's import-competing industries, its exporters will gain from improved market access abroad if all countries reduce tariff barriers simultaneously. The larger the number of countries and the coverage of sectors, the bigger are the potential gains from multilateral trade negotiations.

... and also reduce tariff escalation abroad

Reductions in high MFN tariffs will especially benefit developing country exporters, such as PNG and other Pacific island economies, reliant on agricultural and other primary exports. Developed markets tend to maintain escalating tariff structures that apply higher tariffs to more-processed products. Reducing the degree of tariff escalation abroad will therefore help developing countries to export more processed agricultural products. This will in turn encourage value-added processing in developing countries.

Negotiations also reduce distortions in international commodity markets

A major problem with international commodity markets is that they are heavily distorted by the farm protection measures maintained on certain agricultural products by major countries, especially under the Common Agriculture Policy of the EU and also the USA's Farm Bill. By paying farmers large amounts of domestic support and export subsidies to enable surplus production to be sold on international markets, these policies distort world commodity markets and reduce world prices (Tyers and Anderson 1992). Following the Uruguay Round, multilateral disciplines were introduced for the first time on governments providing such assistance. Reforming these policies will benefit efficient agricultural-exporting countries by allowing world prices to rise towards undistorted levels, at least relative to what otherwise would be the case[27].

Domestic agriculture support payments will be reduced ...

WTO members agreed in the Agriculture Agreement to reduce domestic support payments, as measured by the Total Aggregate Measure of Support, by on average 20% for developed countries and 13.3% for developing countries. Certain subsidies, such as for research and development, are exempted from these reductions if they fall into the so-called 'green box' of payments.

... along with export subsidies

Members also agreed to modestly reduce export subsidies, by on average 36% by value and 21% by volume for developed countries, and by 24% by value and 14% by volume for developing countries.

Disciplines also now apply to quarantine regulations ...

In order to control the use of quarantine arrangements and in particular to limit the possibility that their increased use would frustrate efforts to reduce agricultural protection,

---

[27] That proviso is important. The real price of primary products has been falling about 0.5% per year for the past century on average, so any price increase following trade liberalization would cause a one-off increase in the international price level but the long-run downward trend would then continue — hopefully at a bit slower pace though, as newly industrializing countries will now not be able to follow the costly example of more advanced economies switching from taxing to subsidizing agriculture in the course of their economic development (Anderson 1995).

members negotiated the Sanitary and Phytosanitary (SPS) Agreement. This provides that while members are perfectly entitled to apply quarantine regulations to protect health and safety, they have to provide scientific justification based on an acceptable (rather than zero) degree of risk where their standards differ from international norms. Moreover, such regulations may not be used as disguised restrictions on trade.

... which may be a mixed blessing for developing countries

The SPS Agreement thus can be beneficial for developing countries that have found it difficult to penetrate excessive quarantine barriers to their food exports to other countries in the past. It was partly because of a fear that such barriers might be used more as WTO members bring down their traditional import barriers that the SPS Agreement was negotiated in the first place. Offsetting this beneficial effect, however, is the flipside of this new WTO right, namely, that developing countries have a new obligation to abide by the SPS rules themselves. In so far as PNG and other Pacific island economies have SPS import barriers, they will need to demonstrate that those measures have been applied in a consistent and least-trade-distorting way[28]. Given their relatively weaker administrative capacity, numerous poorer countries are finding implementation of this agreement difficult. PNG is apparently among them, as its National Agriculture Quarantine Inspection Authority (NAQIA) is struggling to meet this aspect of the nation's WTO obligations. PNG does maintain stringent quarantine regulations on certain food imports, including import bans, which may well not be scientifically justified (WTO 1999). It would be in PNG's own economic interests to review its quarantine regulations to ensure that they were scientifically justified and not being used as a de facto trade restriction.

---

[28] It is widely reported among the business community in PNG that the quarantine regulations applied by NAQIA are a significant barrier to imports. Although the arrangements are unclear, it appears that PNG maintains blanket prohibitions on many vegetables and fruits that can be grown domestically, and it would seem highly unlikely that these could be justified on scientific grounds. Rather, they serve as a covert form of economic protectionism.

Improved market access for agricultural exports is materializing...

The region's exports face considerable barriers in their main export markets, including EU, USA, Japan, Australia, New Zealand, Thailand, Malaysia and China (ESCAP 2000). The main barriers are found on agricultural exports which, apart from fish and logs plus oils and minerals from PNG, comprise most of the region's exports. And many of those barriers involve quarantine regulations to protect human, animal or plant health, or food safety standards (Table 5.1).

... via relaxation of quarantine regulations abroad

All WTO members are required to relax their SPS regulations where they are more stringent than international norms, unless those measures can be scientifically justified based on an acceptable degree of risk that is consistently applied. This means that PNG and other Pacific island economies could challenge within the WTO quarantine regulations any major export markets that were considered to be unnecessarily stringent and hurting their export interests.

... and reduced distortions to markets for commodities of key export interest to the Pacific

Given the vital importance of agriculture to the economic prosperity of PNG and other Pacific island economies, depressed world commodity prices resulting from distorted markets are likely to undermine their export interests. A good example is tropical oil products, such as copra, coconut and oil palm in which PNG, the Solomon Islands and other regional economies have a major export interest.

These governments believe that competition from EU subsidised vegetable oils are hurting island economies by further lowering world prices for tropical edible oil products (WTO 1998, WTO 1999). If PNG and other Pacific island economies are going to successfully achieve their development potential, much of which initially must come from the agricultural sector, their prospects would be boosted considerably by the removal of price-depressing distortions in world commodity markets of interest. While the disciplines on agricultural subsidies currently in place are only modest, they provide at least some coverage by the WTO and thereby some constraint on the use of such measures. The challenge confronting all WTO members is to strengthen the agricultural rules in future negotiations. Meeting that challenge will be of direct benefit to Pacific island states.

Table 5.1: Major non-tariff measures affecting exports from Pacific island economies (continued)

Non-tariff measure	Exports affected	Major exporters	Importing country with measures
Product characteristic requirements to protect human health	Fish, meat preparations, cereal foods, fruit & vegetables, sugar, coffee, cocoa, spices, food preparations, hides skins, copra, palm nuts, logs, perfume & cosmetics, starch, wood products, electrical machinery, zoo & animal pets, animal materials	Fiji, Micronesia, Kiribati, Marshall Islands, PNG, Solomon Islands, Tonga, Cook Islands, Vanuatu, Samoa, Niue, Tuvalu	Japan, Australia, Thailand, EU
Import prohibition to protect animal or plant life (dolphins, sea turtles)	Fish, animal & vegetable material	Fiji, Micronesia, Kiribati, Marshall Islands, PNG, Solomon Islands	US, Singapore
Non-automatic import licensing	Fish, meat preparations, fruit & vegetables, vegetable oils, animal materials	Fiji, Micronesia, Kiribati, Marshall Islands, PNG, Solomon Islands, Cook Islands, Vanuatu, Samoa, Niue	Japan, EU, Singapore
Food standards	Cereal foods	Fiji	Australia
Automatic import licensing	Fruit & vegetables, nuts	Tonga, Cook islands, Vanuatu, Samoa, Niue, Fiji	EU, Singapore

Table 5.1: Major non-tariff measures affecting exports from Pacific island economies

Non-tariff measure	Exports affected	Major exporters	Importing country with measures
Labeling requirements to protect human health	Beef, fish, cereal foods, fruit & vegetables, sugar, coffee, spices, palm nuts, vegetable oils, starch, zoo and animal pests	Vanuatu, Fiji, Tonga, Cook Islands, Samoa, Niue, Kiribati, Marshall Islands, PNG, Solomon Islands, Tuvalu	Japan, Australia
Testing, inspection & quarantine requirements	Beef, cereal foods, fruit & vegetables, nuts, coffee	Vanuatu, Fiji, Micronesia, Kiribati, Marshall Islands, PNG, Solomon Islands, Tonga, Cook Islands, Samoa, Niue	Japan, US, Australia, Malaysia, Philippines
Import quotas/tariff quotas	Beef, fish, fruit & vegetables, sugar, coffee, food preparations, starch	Vanuatu, Tonga, Cook Islands, Samoa, Niue, Fiji, Tuvalu	EU, US, Japan, China, Malaysia, Korea
Production/export subsidies	Beef, cereal foods, sugar	Vanuatu, Fiji	EU, US
Licensing for sensitive products	Fish, petroleum	Fiji, Micronesia, Kiribati, Marshall Islands, PNG, Solomon Islands	Australia
Prior import authorization (CITES)	Fish, meat preparations, coffee, vegetable oils, hides & skins, palm nuts, zoo & animal pets, animal materials	Fiji, Micronesia, Kiribati, Marshall Islands, PNG, Solomon Islands, Tonga, Vanuatu, Samoa	EU, Japan, Singapore, Malaysia

Table 5.1: Major non-tariff measures affecting exports from Pacific island economies (continued)

Non-tariff measure	Exports affected	Major exporters	Importing country with measures
Variable charges	Fruit & vegetables	Tonga, Cook Islands, Vanuatu, Samoa, Niue, Fiji	Japan, EU
Import licensing for normally prohibited goods	Sugar, coffee	Fiji, PNG, Solomon Islands, Tonga, Vanuatu	Malaysia
Licensing for selected purchasers	Sugar, logs, petroleum	Fiji, PNG, Solomon Islands, Vanuatu	China
Import inspection	Sugar, vegetable oils, cocoa, logs, petroleum, perfume & cosmetics, electrical machinery	Fiji, PNG, Solomon Islands, Tonga, Vanuatu, Tuvalu, Samoa	China
Technical measures	Cocoa, electrical machinery	PNG, Solomon Islands, Tonga, Vanuatu, Samoa	Japan, Australia
Prior authorization for political reasons	Logs	Fiji, PNG, Solomon Islands, Vanuatu	Japan
Administrative pricing	Logs, petroleum	Fiji, PNG, Solomon Islands, Vanuatu	China
Prohibition	Zoo & animal pets	Solomon Islands	China
Retrospective surveillance	Clothing	Fiji	EU

Source: ESCAP (2000).

These governments believe that competition from EU subsidised vegetable oils are hurting island economies by further lowering world prices for tropical edible oil products (WTO 1998, WTO 1999). If PNG and other Pacific island economies are going to successfully achieve their development potential, much of which initially must come from the agricultural sector, their prospects would be boosted considerably by the removal of price-depressing distortions in world commodity markets of interest. While the disciplines on agricultural subsidies currently in place are only modest, they provide at least some coverage by the WTO and thereby some constraint on the use of such measures. The challenge confronting all WTO members is to strengthen the agricultural rules in future negotiations. Meeting that challenge will be of direct benefit to Pacific island states.

Fish and logs are important resources, yet are subject to weak multilateral disciplines

Such products as fish and logs are important for PNG and several other Pacific island economies. However, unprocessed fish and logs are not covered by the WTO's agricultural agreement, and so multilateral disciplines in these areas are weak. This may be a major problem in fishing, where it has been claimed that Pacific fishing vessels cannot compete with Asian and European fishing fleets which are heavily subsidized by governments (Grynberg 1998). It would be in the economic (and environmental) interests of the region, therefore, to have multilateral disciplines extended in the WTO to cover fishing so as to control such subsidies. Providing matching subsidies to their domestic fleets, even if financially possible, does not make economic sense for the Pacific islands, as these would only compound the economic costs that distorted foreign policies are imposing on island economies.

Keeping market access abroad in proper perspective

Securing improved market access abroad is insufficient ...

While obtaining improved market access abroad is important for the export interests of PNG and other Pacific island economies, such gains must be kept in proper perspective. Improved access only provides an opportunity to increase export penetration to those markets. Whether that opportunity is realized depends entirely on whether the island economies are competitive world suppliers of such products. If not, then the benefits of improved MFN access to overseas markets will accrue instead to more competitive exporters.

... because international competitive-ness and efficiency also require sound policies at home

The capacity of Pacific island economies to compete internationally is determined to a considerable extent by policies at home. Export penetration in foreign markets ultimately depends upon being internationally competitive. If industries are not competitive, no amount of market access abroad will improve their trade and economic performance. The main factors inhibiting exports of Pacific island nations are their own policies. Import-restrictive measures are one source, − since tariffs and other import barriers ultimately tax exports.[29] Another source is macro-economic imbalance, which raises interest rates, reduces capital formation and generally contributes to an inefficient economy. These policies, together with governance and institutional weaknesses as well as poor infrastructure, debilitate the functioning of the private sector. It is these severe 'supply-side' constraints that are the main obstacle to growth, rather than limitations on access to foreign markets.

---

[29] See Clements and Sjaastad (1984) for an excellent explanation of this crucial but not-intuitively-obvious point. In this protective respect Pacific island economies are not unlike many other natural resource-rich economies (see Anderson 1998), but that is no reason to continue with an anti-trade, anti-primary sector policy bias.

Benefits from trade liberalization arise mainly from improved market access at home

Smaller countries like PNG and Pacific island economies would benefit from liberalizing their own markets for imports irrespective of whether or not other nations followed. Opening up domestic markets to cheaper imports makes those markets more competitive and enhances the nation's productivity and economic efficiency by improving resource allocation and the efficiency of using imported intermediate inputs. The most effective means of overcoming foreign exchange shortages is to raise exports and attract capital inflow. Enhanced export and investment performance by small economies does not depend on achieving improved market access abroad, helpful though that may be.

This will become increasingly so as tariff preference margins are reduced

On-going multilateral tariff reductions will continue to place greater competitive pressures on all countries, including developing WTO members. Even if a developing country maintains its own trade barriers against imports, its exports will come under increasing competition in export markets for at least two reasons. One is that other developing countries supplying those same markets are becoming more competitive as they reform their own markets. The second reason is that Lome and other preferential tariff margins are being eroded by the MFN tariff cuts of developed countries. Thus, being able to raise the international competitiveness of their industries will be of increasing importance, and this will require substantial economic reforms at home, including trade liberalization.

Providing special treatment for developing countries in WTO

WTO applies special and differential treatment to DCs ...

In addition to receiving the standard benefits above of WTO membership, developing and especially least-developed country members also are entitled to special treatment in the WTO. This manifests itself in many ways throughout the agreements and operations of the WTO, but generally falls under the term 'special and differential treatment' (S&D) for developing country members.

... which takes many forms

Under S&D, developing countries are generally required to make lower market access commitments and are allowed longer transitional periods to meet new obligations. For example, developing countries have ten years within which to implement progressively the requirements of the WTO Agreement on Agriculture, instead of six years as for developed economies. Similarly, developing countries were treated more leniently in commitments on tariff reductions[30]. In many areas, WTO requirements for developing, and especially least-developing, members are very minimal, ostensibly in order to reflect their stage of development.

But economic benefits of such special treatment are likely to be small and short term at best

While such special treatment in the form of providing them with much longer transitional periods to implement WTO commitments may be needed for political reasons, the perceived economic benefits of also allowing them to negotiate much lower liberalization commitments may be largely illusory and short term at best. For reasons advanced elsewhere in this report, it is equally imperative that all countries, irrespective of their stage of development, reform for their own sake their policies at home so as to boost their productivity, exports and economic growth. Thus, developing countries that overly rely on access to such S&D treatment as a reason for not liberalizing their own economies are likely in the longer run to be undermining their own economic growth prospects.

DCs should recognize that S&D treatment is not without cost

Thus, PNG and other Pacific island countries should be aware of the potential costs to their own economy of overly relying on special and differential treatment. Such treatment as excessively 'watered down' liberalization commitments involve the greatest costs, certainly compared to measures that provide them with longer transition periods. The new agreements negotiated during Uruguay Round acknowledged this by to some extent placing greater emphasis on providing S&D via longer transitional periods instead of reduced commitments.

---

[30] See UNCTAD (1997, Annex 2) for a comprehensive listing of areas providing special treatment for developing countries.

Transparency and monitoring members' trade policies

Good trade policy is underpinned by transparency

Protectionist trade policies partly exist because of a lack of domestic transparency as to the effects of such policies. Because trade barriers benefit certain segments of the community while penalizing others, it is necessary that the effects of such measures be transparent so that the winners and losers of trade reforms or protection can be identified.

Transparency helps redress systemic bias towards granting protection

Without such transparency, there is bound to be a bias in the system towards governments providing protection. The costs to special groups adversely affected by trade reforms will be visible and short term, while the winners will be diverse, less obvious and may have to wait a long time to reap benefits from phased reform. Thus, transparency is needed as a means of redressing this bias towards providing protection, and to enable an informative public dialogue to occur between all affected parties, including consumers. Governments have an important role in providing this transparency and information. Put simply, transparency is imperative for good policy making.

Protection should not be provided 'behind closed doors', but based on public criteria

Providing domestic industries with protection should be based on public and transparent criteria that take account of national welfare rather than narrow sectoral interests. Thus, governments should avoid making special deals behind closed doors with certain industries that are sure to be motivated by their vested interests. Domestic industries wanting assistance should be required to publicly justify why it is more worthy of government support than some other activity since, by definition, all forms of government support inevitably discriminate between activities. Thus, while it is important that governments consult widely with all community groups, governments in the end must make decisions on protection with national welfare in mind.

Transparency primarily works in the government's favour

Governments often feel that greater transparency of its own policies is disadvantageous because it provides other governments with 'ammunition' (information) with which to attack its own policies both bilaterally and multilaterally. Thus, many governments have a double standard to greater transparency: they demand greater transparency of other countries' trade policies, but become defensive when it comes to themselves providing greater transparency. Governments are frequently also reluctant to increase transparency at home because it places greater disciplines on their own actions and exposes policies to public scrutiny. But doing so helps control corrupt practices by politicians and senior policymakers by ensuring that special deals between government and private sector participants are motivated by national welfare concerns and not by vested interests. For these reasons, even though many governments often see transparency as their enemy rather than an effective ally for good governance and policy making, the opposite is true.

Transparency exposes poor policies

If a country's policies are inconsistent with its multilateral commitments or run counter to national welfare objectives, then they need to be identified so that these policies can be amended. Of course, this touches heavily on political considerations. But at the end of the day, economic growth is the means by which governments advance national welfare, and exposing poor policies is part of the required strategy for mazimizing that growth.

WTO's Trade Policy Review Mechanism (TPRM)

WTO can help alleviate the shortfall in national transparency

Thanks to the Uruguay Round, the TPRM has provided the WTO with an effective means of enhancing transparency of members' trade policies. Although concerned mainly with improving international transparency or understanding of members' trade policies and their adherence to commitments and rules in order to improve the functioning of the multilateral system, it nevertheless can make a significant contribution to domestic transparency[31]. Members are to be reviewed continuously every two, four or six years, depending on their share of world trade[32].

The TPRM recognizes the value of domestic transparency

In creating the TPRM, members recognized the inherent value of domestic transparency of government decision-making on trade policy for both their own economies and the multilateral trading system. Members therefore agreed to encourage and promote greater transparency within their own systems on a voluntary basis, taking account of each member's legal and political systems.

TPRM is best seen as an independent external audit of a member's trade–related policies

Reviews are conducted by WTO members in the Trade Policy Review Body (effectively the WTO Council under another name). It is thus a peer review that is based on two reports, one by the member under review and the other and more detailed report prepared by the WTO Secretariat on its own responsibility. Both the reports together with the review meetings' deliberations are published by the Secretariat in the interests of transparency. The reviews cover trade-related policies and hence are much broader in coverage than WTO matters, and include the members' macro-economic setting as well as all aspects of structural policies, such as investment, exchange rates and privatization. However, the main focus is on trade policies.

---

[31] The TPRM is not, however, a legal exercise and has no dispute settlement role. It is not intended to serve as a basis for the enforcement of specific obligations or to impose new policy commitments on members. It is primarily an economic review aimed at examining the impact on the economy of members' trade-related policies.

[32] The top four trading entities within the WTO (EU, USA, Japan and Canada) are reviewed every two years; the next 16 most important world traders every four years; and all other members every six years, with the possibility of longer intervals for the poorest developing country members.

The PNG, Fiji and Solomon Islands TPRs expressed wide policy concerns

Pacific island economies are on a 6-year review cycle. The three current WTO members have been reviewed once: Fiji in 1997; Solomon Islands in 1998; and PNG in 1999. While these reviews supported and welcomed the trade liberalization efforts by respective governments, members expressed a number of reservations over key policy measures (Box 5.4). For example, the PNG review expressed concerns on matters such as PNG's remaining relatively high tariffs; export policies; quarantine regulations; public sector corruption; and the deteriorating business climate, including the serious law and order problem.

PNG needs to resurrect its national transparency agency

PNG has had an independent statutory body, the Industry Assistance Board (IAB), since 1985 to advise the government on industry assistance. However, the IAB has never effectively operated because of a lack of government support and institutional capacity. One of the most effective actions that could be taken would be for the government to resurrect this board so as to make it a more effective national transparent agency. This would facilitate the operations of the Consultative Implementation and Monitoring Council (CIMC) and should become the government's principal source of independent advice on government assistance and regulations. The Board's legislation requires it to apply an economy-wide or national welfare framework in reviewing such policies, and hence could help provide public scrutiny of policies. It could effectively identify the winners and losers from protection, and would make such decisions on providing support to privileged sectors more open and transparent.

Box 5.4: Trade Policy Reviews of Pacific Island Economies

Three pacific island economies have been reviewed under the WTO Trade Policy Review Mechanism. The following provides a brief summary of the Chairperson's Concluding Remarks for each of these meetings.

Papua New Guinea

WTO members emphasized the importance of improved economic management and government in enhancing PNG's economic performance, and welcomed the Government's renewed commitment to trade liberalization and further economic reforms aimed at improving the economy's productivity. They welcomed the bold tax reform package from 1 July 1999, including the reduction in average tariffs from 20% to 9%, and efforts taken to restore fiscal discipline and macro-economic stability. PNG was encouraged to press ahead with the Structural Reform program with the collaboration of the World Bank and IMF, including privatization of state-owned enterprises and liberalization of foreign investment policies. However, members queried a number of areas, including:

-notifications to the WTO;

-high applied tariffs, a few of which appear to exceed bound rates, and some rate increases under the reform program;

-tariffs and other policies designed to promote fisheries and food processing;

-impact of regional trade initiatives;

-export policies, including taxes on logs;

-custom valuation procedures, especially the use of the fallback value method;

-the impact of PNG standards and testing procedures on imports, as well as stringent quarantine restrictions and bans on animals, fruit and vegetables;

-the lack of significant intellectual property legislation and enforcement;

-limited GATS commitments in services;

-the privatization process, especially of key utilities, such as electricity, telecommunications and transport sectors;

-distorting effects of continued price controls;

Box 5.4: Trade Policy Reviews of Pacific Island Economies (cont.)
-participation in the Government Procurement Agreement;
-competition policy;
-public sector corruption; and
-the deteriorating business climate, including the serious law and order problem.
The Solomon Islands
Members appreciated the difficulties faced by the Solomon Islands as a vulnerable non-diversified economy affected by external shocks. They welcomed the efforts by the Government to implement economic reforms, including tariff rationalization, and efforts to conform to WTO commitments. Members queried several areas, including:
-remaining high and disparate tariffs, including the 'temporary' imposition of a 10% tariff surcharge in 1998 without time limits;
-the effectiveness and desirability of using export taxes and other controls to encourage downstream processing of logs and fish;
-effects of MFN liberalization on Lome and other preferences;
-the adverse impact of export subsidies on oilseeds by other members;
-support and membership of regional trading arrangements; and
-the role on investment incentives and non-transparent foreign investment regulations.
Fiji
Members welcomed Fiji's moves since 1989 to adopt more outward-oriented policies, including the elimination of import quotas and tariff reductions. However, concerns were raised in several areas, including:
-the slowing pace of tariff reform and import liberalization;
-relative high and disparate tariffs on some products, such as fish, combined with
-considerable duty escalation and use of specific duties;
-support and membership of regional trading arrangements;
-sanitary and phytosanitary regulations; and
-importance of services, especially tourism
Source: WTO (1997, 1998b and 1999).

It would also help political and community ownership of trade reforms

Reform policies externally imposed on governments are less likely to be successful because they lack strong political or community support. This is probably a major reason why in the past the conditional reform programs of the World Bank and the IMF have occasionally stalled in PNG, the Solomon Islands and many other developing economies. Reform policies must be internally driven and have broad political and community support. A well functioning Industry Assistance Board could help build such support.

WTO notification requirements

Notifications aid transparency

Most WTO agreements require members to regularly provide, either bi-annually or annually, comprehensive notifications to the WTO of existing measures and of any changes. These notifications under various WTO committees are circulated to all members by the Secretariat and made public on its website[33]. They therefore provide an essential means by which members communicate to each other on their trade policies and measures. Notification requirements for PNG are summarized in Table 5.2. Some of these requirements involve the provision of trade regulations and measures for circulation to all members.

Enquiry points also help

Many agreements also require members to notify to the WTO enquiry points that overseas traders or officials can contact to obtain information on a country's trade policies and measures. These facilitate transparency and foreign understanding of a country's trade policies and measures. In the process, they aid domestic transparency too.

Compliance costs of WTO membership

Having discussed the benefits to PNG and other Pacific island economies of WTO membership, it is important to examine whether there are any compliance costs.

---

[33] See the WTO homepage at http://www.wto.org.

Loss of government sovereignty over policies

Is national sovereignty eroded by WTO membership?

It is often argued that a major cost of WTO membership is that governments lose sovereignty over making their own policies and that the WTO imposes policies on members which may not be in each members' interests. This is often argued, for example, by those that are concerned with the perceived effects of freer trade and globalization on environmental protection.

WTO assists governments to follow sound economic policies

However, such concerns are largely misinformed. The WTO has no independent power. The WTO is in fact a secretariat only; it is the member governments that agree, for example, to negotiate the various multilateral trade agreements. Those agreements provide wide scope for

Table 5.2 Notifications to the WTO by PNG as at 30 June 1999

WTO Agreement	Description of requirement	Periodicity	Status as at August 1999 and document number of latest notification
Agriculture (Art. 18.2)	Domestic support	Annual	Outstanding
Agriculture (Art. 10 and 18.2)	Export subsidies (outlays and quantities)	Annual	Outstanding
Subsidies (Art. 32)	Laws and regulations	Once by March 1995, then changes	Outstanding
Subsidies (Art. 25)	Specific subsidies granted	Annual	Outstanding
Subsidies (Art. 25.11)	Countervailing duty actions taken	Every six months when measure is taken	No notification received
Anti-dumping (Art. 18)	Laws and regulations	Once by March 1995, then changes	Outstanding
Anti-dumping (Art. 16.4)	Anti-dumping actions taken	Every six months preliminary or final anti-dumping actions	No notification received
Safeguards (Art. 12)	Laws and regulations	Once by March 1995, then changes	Outstanding
Safeguards (Art. 12)	Investigations and actions taken	Ad hoc	No notification received

Source:

Table 5.2 Notifications to the WTO by PNG as at 30 June 1999 (continued)

WTO Agreement	Description of requirement	Periodicity	Status as at August 1999 and document number of latest notification
Trade-related Investment Measures	Notifications under Article 6.2 of the TRIMS agreement of publications in which TRIMS may be found	By February 1997 or upon membership	Outstanding
GATT 1994 (Part IV)	Enabling Clause	Ad hoc	No notifications received
GATT Council of Trade in Goods on State Trading (Art. XVII:4(a))	State trading entities and activities	Annual	Outstanding
GATT Council for Trade in Goods, G/L/59	Complete notifications on non-tariff measures	Every two years, beginning January 1996	Outstanding
GATS (Art. 3.1)	Alterations to rules governing scheduled sectors	Annual	No notification received
TRIPS (Art. 63.2)	Laws and regulations	Once, then changes	Outstanding: IP/N/1/PNG/1, 21/07/1998
TRIPS (Art. 63.2)	Arrangements for patent protection on pharmaceutical and/or agricultural chemicals	Ad hoc, but only if patent protection on these goods not already granted	No notification received

Source: WTO (1999).

Table 5.2 Notifications to the WTO by PNG as at 30 June 1999 (continued)

WTO Agreement	Description of requirement	Periodicity	Status as at August 1999 and document number of latest notification
Technical Barriers to Trade (Art. 15.2)	Administrative arrangements taken to implement Agreement	Once by March 1995, then changes	Outstanding
Preshipment Inspection (Art. 5)	Laws and regulations that put the Agreement into force	Once, then changes only	Outstanding
Import Licensing Procedures (Art 7.3)	Questionnaire; rules and information concerning procedures for the submission of applications	Annual for questionnaire; rules and information once, then changes	Outstanding; G/LIC/N/2/PNG/1, 24/07/1998
Import Licensing Procedures (Art.1.4(a) and 8.2 (b))	Laws and regulations relevant to import licensing	Once, then changes only	Outstanding
Customs Valuation (Arts. 20.1 and 22.1)	Delay in commencement of provisions and changes in laws	Once on delay, then changes only	Outstanding
Rules of Origin (Art. 5.1 and Annex II, para. 4)	Preferential and non-preferential rules of origin	Non-preferential in April 1995; preferential as soon as entry into force	Outstanding

members to exercise their own trade and other economic policies, as is illustrated by the very diverse and often protectionist policies maintained across the membership. Moreover, efforts to strengthen the multilateral disciplines and to broaden their coverage, while at the same time ensuring greater compliance from members, are best seen as helping all governments to follow sound policies that will maximize national welfare of each member and be mutually beneficial.

Financial and other resource costs

WTO membership does have some costs

Complying and servicing the WTO requires non-trivial resource costs. This is especially so in relative terms for small developing economies, such as PNG and other Pacific island economies. One concern is that the WTO may distract Pacific island economies from pursuing unilateral reforms. However, as argued in this report, if used correctly WTO membership can reinforce unilateral reforms. The greater risk comes from regional trading initiatives, as they consume the limited bureaucratic capacities of Pacific island economies and distract attention away from unilateral and multilateral trade reforms. To some extent, disenchantment with the more-distant MFN system is always likely to spur greater interest in regional arrangements (hence the need to ensure that the multilateral system is working well).

Direct financial costs are small ...

The direct cost of running the WTO, amounting to about SF130 million annually, is funded by members based on their size as traders. Industrialized economies therefore meet most of these costs. For example, the annual financial contribution of PNG and other Pacific island economies is relatively small (no more than SF50,000 annually).

... while indirect costs are larger ...

However, the indirect costs of servicing WTO membership are likely to be much higher. This requires sending officials to the WTO and maintaining some sort of representation in Geneva. It also requires a considerable number of officials in capital cities to work on servicing the multilateral requirements. Not surprisingly, therefore, PNG and other Pacific island economies so far have not been active participants in the GATT/WTO. One way to lower the cost of participating is to pool resources though. To that end, the (South Pacific) Forum Secretariat is examining the prospects of establishing a joint mission to the WTO in Geneva to represent Pacific island members.

... including costs of notification

Meeting the notification and transparency costs of WTO membership can also be costly in terms of its use of direct and indirect resources. However, these costs are almost certainly going to be insignificant compared to the social benefits nationally of improved policy making and enhanced trading. Put starkly, active participation in the WTO and meeting its transparency and monitoring requirements probably could make the greatest contribution to facilitating trade.

Adjustment costs of implementing WTO- (and APEC-) consistent policies

Costs of adjustment to reform are non-trivial ...

The restructuring costs to the economy of implementing WTO- (and thereby also APEC-) consistent policies are often seen as the major compliance costs of such membership. Replacing inward-looking protectionist policies with open and outward-looking trade and investment policies obviously imposes some short-term adjustment costs on the economy. However, the costs to the economy of not making these changes and persisting with past protectionist policies are far greater. Structural adjustment is always occurring in any economy. Protection simply transfers the burden of adjustment onto efficient industries. Trade liberalization redresses this imbalance by placing the pressure of adjustment where it should be, namely on inefficient industries.

... but they are one-off costs, unlike the benefits, which are ongoing

Adjustment costs induced by policy reforms are therefore best viewed not as on-going costs of compliance with the WTO, but rather as one-off costs associated with unwinding past policy mistakes in order to gain from the longer-term benefits of trade liberalization and economic growth. It must be remembered that while the adjustment costs are immediate they are only short term, while the benefits of reform continue to be received perpetually. Thus, compliance costs are not so much associated with WTO membership as with implementing sensible economic policies. To not do so imposes larger, albeit less visible, costs on efficient producers from having to cope with unsound policies.

PNG trade policies generally comply with WTO requirements ...

PNG trade policies generally comply with its WTO commitments. The tariff reform program will reduce tariffs to a maximum of 40% by 2006, thereby meeting its WTO tariff bindings. It had already removed non-tariff measures covered by the WTO and, with the possible exception of quarantine regulations, appears to have policies that broadly comply with WTO commitments − provided the reform program is implemented. PNG has therefore already taken the necessary steps to meet its key obligations. The same generally applies to Fiji and the Solomon Islands.

... but reform commitments could be strengthened

However, while PNG and other Pacific island members of the WTO significantly expanded their commitments in the Uruguay Round, they remain relatively modest compared to the reform opportunities remaining in these countries. Thus, governments should not only look at meeting their WTO commitments, but also overtaking them unilaterally. For those Pacific island economies currently undergoing WTO accession, this process itself can provide an effective means of reforming economic policies and locking these in internationally through WTO membership.

Commitment weaknesses include services ...

PNG, Fiji and the Solomon Islands generally undertook minimal commitments on services under the General Agreement on Trade in Services (GATS). Virtually no liberalization commitments were made, although in a few sectors, such as certain banking services, PNG and the Solomon Islands did commit to continuing to maintain no limitations on market access and national treatment for services supplied cross-border, consumed abroad and by commercial presence (Tables 5.3 and 5.4). The main liberalizing commitment was in telecommunications where PNG did commit to removing the current statutory monopoly held by Telikom PNG over basic communications from 2002. PNG also adopted the regulatory principles for telecommunications thereby committing to ensure that, from then on, foreign suppliers would be able to interconnect with the local network in a non-discriminatory manner. Many of these requirements are contained in the Telecommunications Act of 1996 that established PANGTEL as the sole regulatory and licensing authority for telecommunications.

Table 5.3 Summary of sector-specific commitments by PNG under the WTO General Agreement on Trade in Services (GATS)

Sector or subsector	Modes of supply			
	Cross-border supply	Consumpti on abroad	Commercial presence	Temporary presence of natural persons[a]
	Market access (MA)/national treatment (NT)			
Tourism & Related Services				
Hotels & restaurants (including catering)	None (MA & NT)	None (MA & NT)	None (MA & NT	Unbound (MA & NT), subject to horizontal limitation
Transport Services				
Maritime, passenger & freight	None (MA & NT)	None (MA & NT)	None (MA & NT)	Unbound (MA & NT), subject to horizontal limitation
Financial Services				
Banking & other financial services (excluding insurance); retail deposit acceptance, lending, financial leasing, guarantees & commitments & trading (including in money market instruments, foreign exchange & transferable securities	None (MA & NT)	None (MA & NT)	None (MA & NT)	Unbound (MA & NT), subject to horizontal limitation
Construction & Related Engineering Services				

Sector or subsector	Modes of supply			
	Cross-border supply	Consumption abroad	Commercial presence	Temporary presence of natural persons[a]
	Market access (MA)/national treatment (NT)			
General construction work for buildings	Unbound (MA & NT) due to technical feasibility	None (MA & NT)	None (MA); NT exception to prefer national firms for construction contracts under K 500,000.	Unbound (MA & NT), subject to horizontal limitation
General construction work for civil engineering	Unbound (MA & NT) due to technical feasibility	None (MA & NT)	None (MA); NT exception to prefer national firms for construction contracts under K 500,000	Unbound (MA & NT), subject to horizontal limitations
Business Services Professional services				
- Legal services	None (MA & NT)	None (MA & NT)	None (MA & NT)	Unbound (MA & NT), subject to horizontal limitation
- Accounting, auditing & bookkeeping services	None (MA & NT)	None (MA & NT)	None (MA & NT)	Unbound (MA & NT), subject to horizontal limitation

Sector or subsector	Modes of supply			
	Cross-border supply	Consumpti on abroad	Commercial presence	Temporary presence of natural persons[a]
	Market access (MA)/national treatment (NT)			
- Architectural services	None (MA & NT)	None (MA & NT)	None (MA & NT)	Unbound (MA & NT), subject to horizontal limitations
- Engineering services	None (MA & NT)	None (MA & NT)	None (MA & NT)	Unbound (MA & NT), subject to horizontal limitation
Computer & related services	None (MA & NT)			
- Consultancy services on hardware installation	None (MA & NT)	None (MA & NT)	None (MA & NT)	Unbound (MA & NT), subject to horizontal limitation
Other business services				
- management consulting	None (MA & NT)	None (MA & NT)	None (MA & NT)	Unbound (MA & NT), subject to horizontal limitation

Sector or subsector	Modes of supply			
	Cross-border supply	Consumption abroad	Commercial presence	Temporary presence of natural persons[a]
	Market access (MA)/national treatment (NT)			
Communication Services				
Telecommunication				
- voice telephone; packet-switched & circuit-switched data transmission; telex; telegraph; facsimile; private-leased circuit services; digital cellular; paging; personal communication; trunked radio system; & mobile data services	None (NT); MA only using Telikom PNG network – subscribes to regulatory principles	None (NT); MA exception prohibiting alternative calling or call-back	None (NT); MA exception that all services are subject to a five-year exclusivity (1997-2002) to Telikom PNG as monopoly service provider[b]	Unbound (MA & NT), subject to horizontal limitation
- courier services, excluding letters	None (MA & NT)	None (MA & NT)	None (MA & NT)	Unbound (MA & NT), subject to horizontal limitation

a   Horizontal limitation on commercial presence states that market access is subject to normal government approval of foreign investment (and from the Central Bank in the case of financial services) and may only lease land from the government; national treatment requires foreign employees to provide on-the-job training to local employees. For presence of people, market access and national treatment subject to limiting entry of managers and specialists to those of key importance where local employees are unavailable. Entry is limited initially to three years.

b   The issuance of additional operating licences and their terms and conditions will be considered and announced at least two years prior to the end of the exclusivity period. Telikom PNG is designated as signatory to the INTELSAT Operating Agreement. Telikom PNG reserves the right to set up subsidiary companies in business ventures on particular services and telecommunications.

Source: WTO (1999).

Table 5.4 Summary of sector -specific commitments by the Solomon Islands under GATS

Sector or subsector	Modes of supply			
	Cross-border supply	Consumption abroad	Commercial presence	Temporary presence of natural persons
	Market access (ma)/national treatment (nt)			
TOURISM & RELATED SERVICES				
Hotels & restaurants (including catering)	None (ma & nt)	None (ma & nt)	None (ma & nt), subject to horizontal limitation on ma	Unbound (ma & nt), subject to horizontal limitation
FINANCIAL SERVICES				
Banking & other financial services (excluding insurance)	None (ma & nt)	None (ma & nt)	None (ma & nt), subject to horizontal limitation on ma	Unbound, subject to horizontal limitation
All insurance & insurance-related services	None (ma & nt)	(None (ma & nt)	None (ma & nt), subject to horizontal limitation on ma	Unbound, subject to horizontal limitation
CONSTRUCTION & RELATED ENGINEERING SERVICES				
General construction work for buildings	Unbound (ma & nt) due to technical feasibility	None (ma & nt)	None (ma & nt), subject to horizontal limitation on ma	Unbound, subject to horizontal limitation
General construction work for civil engineering	Unbound (ma & nt), except where	None (ma & nt)	None (ma & nt), subject to horizontal limitation on	Unbound, subject to horizontal

	resources and materials are unavailable locally		ma	limitations
BUSINESS SERVICES				
Professional services				
- Legal services, home country law, including public international law	None (ma & nt)	None (ma & nt)	None (ma & nt), except must be sole proprietorship or partnership, and subject to horizontal limitation on ma	Unbound, subject to horizontal limitation
- Accounting, auditing & bookkeeping services	None (ma & nt)	None (ma & nt)	None (ma & nt), subject to horizontal limitation on ma	Unbound, subject to horizontal limitation
- Architectural services	None (ma & nt)	None (ma & nt)	None (ma & nt), subject to horizontal limitation on ma	Unbound, subject to horizontal limitations
- Engineering services	None (ma & nt)	None (ma & nt)	None (ma & nt), subject to horizontal limitation on ma	Unbound, subject to horizontal limitation

Note: Horizontal limitation states that measures are unbound on both market access and national treatment for temporary stay of natural persons, except for key staff with specialist skills not available locally where entry will be limited to two years initially, with any extension subject to immigration and labour laws. Foreign employees are also required to provide on-the-job training to local employees. Horizontal limitations also apply to market-access commitments whereby commercial presence is subject to normal foreign investment, company registration and land ownership requirements.
ma= market access; nt= national treatment

Source: WTO (1998).

... and protection of intellectual property rights

Under the new WTO Agreement on Trade-Related Aspects of Intellectual Property Rights (TRIPS) members were required to implement certain WTO-consistent legislation and enforcement procedures within certain time periods. The transitional period ended in 2000 for developing countries and 2006 for least-developing members. In addition to providing a minimum patent protection period of 20 years, members were to have effective legislation protecting other forms of intellectual property, such as copyright, trademarks as well as industrial and layout designs. In addition, members undertook to ensure effective enforcement of intellectual property rights, including having adequate remedies and seizure powers by customs of counterfeit products.

IP rights and enforcement capacity need strengthening

Pacific island economies, including PNG, Fiji and the Solomon Islands, generally have very weak intellectual property rights and little enforcement capacity. Thus, meeting these requirements will require major changes in legislation, in the courts and in customs operations. However, making such changes has been difficult in view of the countries' technical capacities.

Least-developed economies have longer to comply with TRIPS

PNG and Fiji should have been TRIPS-compliant from 1 January 2000. However, the Solomon Islands, being regarded as a least-developed WTO member, has until 2006. The three island economies currently in the process of acceding to the WTO would need to negotiate such transitional arrangements. Since Vanuatu and Samoa are classified as least-developed economies by the UN, they would be given until 2006 to meet their TRIPS obligations. However, this does not apply to Tonga, since it is not classified as a least-developed economy.

The benefits to island economies of TRIPS compliance are not obvious ...

Achieving TRIPS compliance by small developing economies may impose substantial additional costs on their consumers and may even reduce national welfare. This is because they are technology-importing countries and are likely to remain so for the foreseeable future. By stopping the production and importation of illegal goods infringing property rights, such as pirated music CDs, TRIPS compliance will force consumers to buy the more expensive genuine article. However, against these costs must be set the benefits to such countries of strengthening protection of intellectual property. There is considerable empirical evidence that weak intellectual property protection in host countries is a major deterrent to foreign direct investment. Thus, TRIPS compliance may help stimulate foreign investment in developing countries, and their citizens would also benefit from the greater protection received abroad on any intellectual property developed by them (Maskus 2000).

... but TRIPS was negotiated as part of a larger package for all WTO members to sign ...

TRIPS was incorporated into the WTO during the Uruguay Round largely at the insistence large technology exporting countries, most notable the US. It thus became an important aspect of the negotiated package of WTO commitments that members accepted as a means of trading off particular trading interests. While many developing countries were initially opposed to the inclusion of intellectual property protection in the WTO, they agreed on the basis that this would best serve their overall interests by receiving in return benefits in other areas.

... which included textiles reform

For developing countries, the quid pro quo mainly came in the form of developed countries agreeing to phase-out over 10 years import quotas permitted under the Multi-Fibre Arrangement (MFA). This was seen to be particularly beneficial to developing countries that have a significant export interest in clothing and footwear, including Fiji. This is how the multilateral trade rounds are negotiated; they are broad in coverage to enable members sufficient leeway to trade off their different interests, thereby ensuring that even if certain commitments may not be in their own interests, benefits negotiated in return will produce a package of outcomes that will provide net benefits overall to each member.

6

The supplementary role of APEC

APEC members aim to meet targets on trade and investment liberalization

APEC currently comprises 21 members, following the inclusion of Russia, Vietnam and Peru in 1999. PNG, the only Pacific island economy member, joined APEC in 1994. APEC's initial objective on formation in 1989 of fostering economic cooperation within the Asia Pacific region was expanded to include trade and investment liberalization, following the adoption of the Bogor Declaration in 1994 and the Osaka Action Agenda in 1995. This commits members to achieve free and open trade and investment by 2010 in APEC developed economies, and by 2020 for developing country members.

Unilateral MFN trade liberalization

Unlike with WTO, APEC commitments are voluntary

Such liberalization is to be achieved on a voluntary basis in accordance with Individual Action Plans (IAPs) submitted periodically by each APEC member. These plans should contain specific details of liberalization efforts. Differentiated timetables for achieving the liberalization goals are provided for, to be revised by members on a rolling basis through a progressive consultation process that is reflected in continuous and voluntary improvement of the plans.

... and being non-binding, are more like undertakings

IAPs are not negotiated outcomes nor are they binding on individual members. They can be changed without negotiating compensation with other APEC economies, and there is no formal dispute settlement mechanism. Thus APEC commitments are more akin to undertakings.

Economies are free to vary such plans as they wish. PNG has submitted two IAPs, the first in 1996 and the second in 1998. No new commitments were made in either of its 1996 or 1998 IAPs (PECC 1999). PNG is currently preparing a revised IAP that is due to be finalized in 2000.

Liberalization commitments are comprehensive ...

APEC liberalization is to be comprehensive in that it covers manufacturing, agriculture and services. However, some APEC members, such as Japan and Korea that heavily protect their farmers, are uncomfortable with such comprehensiveness. Any efforts to reduce the product coverage of APEC liberalization would undermine its effectiveness and would go against the interests of PNG which is heavily dependent on agricultural exports. Thus, the PNG Government should strongly support the continued inclusion of agriculture. APEC undertakings cover both tariffs and non-tariff measures.

... and based on 'open regionalism'

A unique aspect of APEC is that trade and investment liberalization is to be non-discriminatory, based on the concept of so-called 'open regionalism'. APEC members are to liberalize on an MFN basis such that non-APEC members will also receive equal access to APEC markets. This is in sharp contrast to a traditional free trade area or customs union whereby members extend tariff preferences to each other and thereby discriminate against countries not party to the agreement.

There is no major 'free rider' problem

Some APEC members, especially the US, have reservations about 'open regionalism' and would prefer a discriminatory agreement as a means of restricting the benefits of liberalization to APEC members. Otherwise, so it is claimed, non-APEC members would be able to 'free ride' on APEC liberalization by receiving the benefits of liberalized export markets without being required to provide improved access to their markets in return. However, such an argument misses two main points. First, it assumes that the economic benefits to APEC members come mainly from receiving improved access abroad for their exports. This is not the case. The benefits of liberalization accrue to each APEC economy predominantly from opening its own markets to imports from the world's most efficient suppliers. Thus, there is really no 'free rider' problem. These benefits accrue from having access to the cheapest imports rather than from obtaining improved market access overseas. And second, in addition to the positive effect of close proximity, the strong complementarity in trade among the APEC countries is such that most of the imports resulting from APEC members opening their economies come from other APEC economies anyway. PNG should therefore support APEC continuing to be an open, outward-looking regional arrangement rather than the alternative of an inward-focused discriminatory trading bloc.

Open regionalism would have been a better model than the Forum's proposed FTA

As mentioned earlier in this report, Forum leaders have endorsed the creation of a discriminatory free trade area between themselves, to start in 2001. However, an alternative and economically superior approach would have been to adopt the APEC model of open regionalism. While this has been rejected to date, the essence of open regionalism could still be encapsulated in the FTA if certain principles were met.

Four conditions would ensure the Forum's FTA facilitates multilateral trade

The key principles that the Forum's FTA should have if it is to boost welfare and facilitate the Pacific island economies' trade multilaterally are:

- full liberalization of trade between parties;

- homogeneous rules of origin across members so as to improve transparency and facilitate external liberalization;

- openness to new members on conditions similar to those available to existing members, with clearly established and transparent procedures for negotiating accession; and

- no increase in external barriers on formation or subsequently, and readiness to negotiate external barrier reductions thereafter (Snape, Adams and Morgan 1993).

Full liberalization of trade between parties is consistent with the APEC comprehensive product coverage approach. Complete internal liberalization will make it easier at a later date to liberalize with the rest of the world. The more goods are exempted from liberalization between partners, the more exceptions will be sought externally. Product-by-product liberalization in regional arrangements has tended to boost trade neither with outsiders nor among the members (Wonnacott and Lutz 1989). Thus, the PNG and other signatories to the FTA should resist the temptation of negotiating to exclude their least-competitive products from liberalization under the agreement.

Future expansion of the Forum's FTA is possible

While the FTA is to be initially formed between FICs, it is important that the decision also calls for an examination of appropriate measures to provide for the application of the FTA to, for example, Australia and New Zealand. In fact the possible longer-term integration of the FTA into the Closer Economic Relations agreement between the latter two countries is already being studied. The expansion of the FTA to include non-Pacific island economies should be encouraged by PNG and other members to ensure that it will deliver maximum gains to them by facilitating wider multilateral liberalization. That would also ensure that all members benefit and not just certain members as is likely to be the case under the current FTA.

APEC in principle goes beyond WTO commitments, but is non-binding on members

APEC's trade and investment liberalization objectives to some extent go beyond those of the WTO, something which the Forum Secretariat might also consider. APEC has adopted 'free and open trade, including services, and investment' as the rule, and has set target dates of either 2010 or 2020 for achieving these goals. No such goals or target dates explicitly exist in the WTO. Moreover, APEC's 'open regionalism' concept and comprehensive product coverage go further than the WTO requirements, which allow for regional FTAs as an exception to MFN treatment provided they apply to 'substantially all trade' and do not raise barriers to third countries. However, APEC's weakness is that such commitments, including the liberalization targets, are non-binding on members.

APEC encompasses unilateral liberalization

Unlike the WTO, which embraces multilateral trade liberalization, APEC is based on unilateral reforms. Members have endorsed the common liberalization targets, but have full autonomy over the reform path pursued to meet these common goals. The approach to trade and investment liberalization is therefore one of 'concerted unilateralism' whereby members continue 'to do their own thing' but in a framework of co-operation and common objectives that will hopefully facilitate greater trade liberalization by all APEC members. Much of the APEC agenda focuses on encouraging members to voluntarily enhance their WTO commitments in both goods and services.

APEC adopted an 'early voluntary sector liberalization' initiative

In order to facilitate accelerated trade liberalization, APEC economies adopted in 1997 the so-called Early Voluntary Sector Liberalization (EVSL) initiative. This aimed at advancing trade liberalization in certain nominated sectors. Members agreed on 15 sectors, of which nine were to be fast-tracked for liberalization. PNG participated in these negotiations and supported other members in the nomination of several sectors for early liberalization, including food, chemicals, and transport equipment. However, the initiative floundered somewhat as several members expressed concerns that it was contrary to the spirit of voluntarism on which APEC was founded. Consequently, APEC economies decided in 1998 to transfer such initiatives to reduce tariffs in these sectors to the WTO. APEC continues to advance liberalization of non-tariff measures in these sectors, but has made little progress to date.

PNG benefits from double membership of WTO and APEC

The success of APEC depends critically on maintaining a strong WTO. APEC members, most of whom (including PNG) also belong to the WTO, have acknowledged that APEC is to be fully compatible with members' multilateral commitments and see APEC primarily as a forum for further advancing unilateral trade reforms within the Asia Pacific region. Thus, any developments that weaken the WTO are likely to have an adverse impact on APEC's success. Belonging to both the WTO and APEC offers the

PNG Government the opportunity to effectively use both to advance its unilateral trade reforms. The WTO provides an effective means of 'locking in' such voluntary reforms undertaken within the APEC context by adding them to PNG's binding multilateral commitments. However, to date most APEC members' IAPs do not reflect the real progress many APEC economies have made toward achieving the Bogor goals (PECC 1999). PNG should be encouraged therefore to include in its updated IAP due this year the current tariff reduction program.

APEC members are encouraged to accelerate their reform commitments

APEC economies are to ensure full and effective implementation of their Uruguay Round outcomes within the agreed time frame in a manner fully consistent with the letter and the spirit of the WTO. Moreover, the goal is that each APEC economy will, on a voluntary basis, accelerate the implementation of Uruguay Round outcomes and deepen and broaden these. Virtually all those APEC economies that are members of the WTO have made explicit commitments in their IAPs to implement their UR obligations (PECC 1999). However, few, if any, APEC members, including PNG, have made commitments that exceed their WTO obligations.

Investment Liberalization

APEC also contains investment initiatives, albeit again non-binding

APEC's Investment Principles are aimed at facilitating unilateral foreign investment reforms within the region to meet the Bogor goal of free and open investment by the specified target dates by members progressively providing for MFN and national treatment as well as ensuring transparency. This contrasts with the WTO, which has no investment agreement, although foreign investment in services is now explicitly covered by the General Agreement on Trade in Services (GATS)[34]. However, APEC

---

[34] By covering commercial presence as one of the four modes of internationally supplying services, WTO members that negotiated bound commitments under GATS for scheduled services had to specify limitations to national treatment and market access provided by their foreign investment regulations. Most members in practice

investment principles are voluntary and non-binding on members.

PNG's investment commitments in APEC are modest, but an important start

By deregulating its investment regime in 1996, PNG is currently phasing out its list of activities reserved for domestic investors, starting with construction and manufacturing. It intends implementing the Business Information Facilitation Center as part of the 'One Stop Shop' Concept. The Government has also commenced the development of a register for foreign investor approvals in conjunction with other related government agencies to facilitate investment. Helpful though these initiatives are, more is needed to attract FDI in a world where this aspect of globalization is accelerating elsewhere.

APEC's investment principles make good economic sense

APEC's non-binding investment principles are themselves modest, and could be strengthened in a number of areas such as requiring limits on the use of investment incentives. They include a number of key properties that foreign investment regimes should meet if they are to be efficient and conducive to economic development. These are:

- Transparency -- all laws, regulations, etc. should be publicly available;

- Non-discrimination between source countries;

- National treatment – foreign investors should be treated no differently than domestic investors;

- Investment incentives – health, safety and environmental regulations should not be relaxed as an incentive to encourage foreign investment;

- Performance requirements – countries should minimize the use of performance requirements that distort or limit the expansion of trade and investment;

---

also provided for a horizontal commitment in their GATS' schedules, specifying that commercial presence on services was subject to their foreign investment laws and regulations.

- Expropriation and compensation – there should be no expropriation of foreign investments, except for a public purpose, and then only with adequate compensation;

- Repatriation and convertibility – the transfer of funds related to foreign investment (profits, dividends, royalties, etc.) should be facilitated and in convertible currencies;

- Settlement of disputes – disputes arising in connection with foreign investment should be settled promptly through consultation and negotiation between the parties or through arbitration procedures acceptable to both parties;

- Entry and sojourn of personal – the temporary entry and sojourn of key foreign technical and managerial personnel connected with foreign investment should be permitted and encouraged, subject to relevant laws and regulations;

- Avoidance of double taxation;

- Behaviour of foreign investors should be consistent with the host country's laws and regulations; and

- Regulatory and institutional barriers to the outflow of investment should be minimized.

Room for much improvement in the Pacific region's investment policies ...

Rules and regulations affecting foreign investment have traditionally been a major problem in Pacific island economies. They have been unnecessarily complex, discretionary and non-transparent, and often impose high transaction costs on investors. Policy statements on foreign investment often have been incomplete and ambiguous, and rules and regulations frequently are applied inconsistently across investors. By contrast, if APEC investment principles were adopted, the environment would be markedly improved.

... as has been recognized in the region's island economies

Non-APEC Pacific island economies could, as with trade, also adopt APEC's investment principles. Indeed FICs have collectively endorsed the pursuit of open, liberal and transparent investment policies consistent with the APEC non-binding investment principles. With this in mind, Forum governments have instituted a process whereby the Forum Secretariat would assess progress among members in bringing national investment policies into line with APEC principles.

Self-assessment of investment regime is dubious

The Forum's initiative has also involved an assessment by individual governments and by the Foreign Investment Advisory Service (FIAS) as to the consistency of their own investment legislation with APEC principles[35]. FIAS reported in 1998 that the countries' self-evaluations of their investment regime showed a high level of compliance and commitment to APEC principles, but warned that these assessments should be treated cautiously. It was likely that the implications of APEC principles were not fully understood by officials and that policy may be incorrectly equated with application. Moreover, regular separate assessments of the transparency of such regulations have also found weaknesses. In the case of PNG, FIAS found considerable departures from the APEC principles, including transparency shortcomings (Tables 6.1).

Investment regimes have plenty of scope for improvement

FIAS has identified several principles as the main ones lacking from the investment regimes of FICs, including PNG, the Solomon Islands and Fiji as well as the other island economies. Repatriation and convertibility as well as temporary entry and sojourn of personnel are two areas where the administrative requirements set are often more onerous than the policy statements would imply. Simplification and increased transparency of the processes would therefore reduce transaction costs faced by investors.

---

[35] FIAS is a joint service of the World bank and the International Finance Corporation.

Table 6.1: Compliance of PNG's investment policies with APEC non-binding principles

APEC non-binding investment principle	Assessment
Transparency	Response not sought
Non-discrimination between source countries	Assessment could not be given based on the information in the response provided
National treatment	Compliance, but with some uncertainty surrounding assessment
Investment incentives	Compliance
Performance requirements	Approaching compliance, but with some uncertainty surrounding assessment
Expropriation and compensation	Assessment could not be given based on the information in the response provided
Repatriation and convertibility	Compliance
Settlement of disputes	Response not sought
Entry and sojourn of personnel	Assessment could not be given based on the information in the response provided
Avoidance of double taxation	Approaching compliance
Interest behaviour	Assessment could not be given based on the information in the response provided
Removal of barriers to capital exports	Approaching compliance, but with some uncertainty surrounding assessment

Source: WTO (1999).

Some positive developments in PNG could be accelerated

Many of the inadequacies in PNG's investment regime are recognized in the Government's National Investment Policy, released in June 1998. The legislative provisions are being reviewed and amendments proposed to the 1992 Investment Promotion Act, which established the Investment Promotion Authority. Legislation is to be amended to re-focus the Authority's role to promote, rather than control, FDI. The new national investment policy is designed to provide transparency, equal treatment, and consistency for investors. It proposes:

- strengthening the Authority's investment support functions by establishing a one-stop shop to process investors more efficiently;

- modifying the Investment Promotion Act to shift from a case-by-case approval process for foreign investments to a simpler system of registration of businesses, with ex post monitoring of investments; and

- reviewing investment procedures under specific sectoral legislation and making the procedures and requirements consistent with a more liberal approach to foreign investment.

PNG's record on foreign investment is not great

Outside the mining sector, PNG has had a disappointing record in attracting foreign investment (Table 6.2). Approvals usually substantially exceed actual levels. This indicates that other factors discourage investors, such as the difficult economic climate as well as policy and political uncertainties that exist in PNG. There may also be considerable obstacles to implementing foreign investment, such as problems in gaining approval from local community groups and obtaining secure land rights. Mining investment, including especially in oil and mineral exploration, also has dropped sharply in recent years.

The planned rationalization of investment incentives is consistent with APEC principles

PNG's National Investment Policy calls for the review of all fiscal and non-fiscal incentives and the development of a comprehensive and transparent framework for providing investment incentives. Investment incentives are to be rationalized under the tax and customs laws. The objective is to formulate a uniform and consistent set of investment incentives that can be administered openly by the Authority. The new arrangements are designed to remove case-by-case ministerial discretion in the use of investment incentives in order to avoid intense lobbying and past misuse.

Table 6.2: Foreign investment approvals in PNG, 1995-98
(K million and per cent)

Sector/Country	1995	1996	1997	1998
Sector				
Agriculture	464	152	7	1
Forestry	398	148	407	40
Mining	1,345	399	501	359
Manufacturing	17	67	232	7
Construction	43	131	282	16
Transport & communication	85	853	72	33
Other	104	169	302	82
Total	*2,456*	*1,919*	*1,803*	*538*
Country (%)[a]				
Australia	21	21	21	17
Malaysia	18	18	18	9
North America	18	18	18	17
China	3	3	3	46
Japan	0.3	0.3	0.3	5
Other Asian crisis economies	3	3	3	2
Other	37	37	37	4

a   Figures for 1995-97 are three-year averages.

Source: WTO (1999).

Other APEC Undertakings

Other APEC undertakings mainly 'back up' WTO disciplines

These areas include standards and conformance; customs procedures; intellectual property rights; and rules of origin. In these cases, APEC undertakings mainly reinforce WTO commitments and thus, for countries such as PNG that are also WTO members, provide few, if any, additional commitments as such, other than the general one of accelerating their implementation where possible (Table 6.3). For example, APEC's commitments on technical standards require members to have transparent standards and conformity assessment procedures that are aligned with international norms in accordance with the WTO Technical barriers to Trade and Sanitary and Phytosanitary Agreements[36]. Similarly, APEC members are committed to implementing the requirements of the WTO Agreements on TRIPS, on rules of origin, on customs valuation, and on services liberalization.

But APEC places additional undertakings on PNG in government procurement

PNG as a non-member of the WTO plurilateral Agreement on Government Procurement is not subject to any multilateral commitments on government procurement to other WTO members. However, APEC's undertakings on government procurement are relevant. These require PNG to develop a common understanding on government procurement policies and systems, and to liberalize its government procurement market in accordance with the principles and objectives of the Bogor Declaration, as well as to contribute in the process to the evolution of work on government procurement in other multilateral fora. An important aspect of this is to enhance the transparency of its government procurement methods.

---

[36] APEC members are also encouraged to enter mutual recognition agreements on standards and conformity testing with APEC economies as provided for in WTO agreements.

Government procurement can become another means of protecting domestic industries

Governments often use public procurement practices to discriminate in favour of domestic suppliers. This can be done explicitly by providing local suppliers with a specified price preference or implicitly by having non-transparent and cumbersome procedures that make it more difficult for foreign suppliers to participate in the procurement process. Such arrangements are highly questionable on efficiency grounds, and risk not only using scare government funds inappropriately but also protecting domestic suppliers against more competitive foreign suppliers. Thus, as a potential form of protection they risk promoting inefficient industries at home that cannot compete without government support. They also provide opportunities for corruption.

Table 6.3: Other PNG APEC commitments

Commitments entered into	Status of implementation
Customs operations	
• Facilitate electronic-data interchange (EDI) communicate and Direct trader Input (DTI) by upgrading ASYCUDA (or similar system) in 1997;	• Adopted the Harmonized tariff system;
• Continue the valuation of goods in accordance with the WTO valuation agreement;	• Assist traders by keeping them informed of any legislative or administrative changes affecting customs operation;
• Conduct training programs to introduce property rights in customs administration once the approval requirements are in place;	• Reviewing Customs Act and Regulations to ensure simplification and harmonization of customs procedures in line with the WCO Kyoto Convention;
• Introduce clearer appeal provisions and review the Customs act and Regulations – change the organizational structure in the Internal Revenue Commission to facilitate better appeal procedures;	• Reviewing ASYCUDA;
• Accede to ATA Convention.	• Reviewing Customs Act and Regulations to allow the introduction of an advance classification ruling system supported by comprehensive training programs.
Standards and conformance	
Short/medium/long term (1998-2020)	
• Adopt international standards on food labeling, electrical appliances, plastic products and rubber;	

Table 6.3: Other PNG APEC commitments (continued)

- Progressively review the implementation of both voluntary and regulatory areas;

- Continue to participate in ISO formulation of international standards and conformity schemes;

- Upgrade the national Institute of Standards and Industrial Technology's capacity and capability;

- Develop its national standard system and metrology system;

- Ensure its membership of other regional bodies;

- Develop National Certification System of Conformity (NCSC);

- Participate ion technical cooperation with APEC member economies on standards and conformance matters;

- Train its exporters, regulatory and testing authorities ton ISO;

- Develop accreditation and certification of regulatory authorities, export testing authorities to ISO, guide 25, 9000 series, 1400 series;

- Sign mutual recognition arrangements in metrology, food, toys and other conformity schemes;

- Does not have widely developed standard procedures and with its membership to APEC has now proceeded to formulate programs to align with international standards;

- Establish database of its National Standards and Technical Regulations;

- Create a database and a network system on (a) standards and conformance systems (b) laboratory accreditation (c) status of mutual recognition agreements (d) status of alignment with international standards.

Table 6.3: Other PNG APEC commitments (continued)

Intellectual property protection

Short/medium/long term (1997-2020)

- Enact copyright and patent laws and review trademarks legislation;
- Continue to provide institutional support to administer and enforce intellectual property rights.

Short/medium/long term (1998-2020)

- Enact the necessary laws for the enforcement of intellectual property rights, including copyright and patent legislation;
- Review Trademark Law;
- Maintain adequate and effective civil and administrative procedures;
- Disseminate information for awareness building.

- Does not have all the necessary laws to protect intellectual property rights except for Trademarks, legislation on which was passed in 1980; evaluating accession to the World Intellectual Property Organization (WIPO); internal consultations held with relevant private and public sector organizations on the establishment of an Intellectual Property Organization tasked to provide and implement enabling legislation as per GATT/WTO requirements under WIPO principles and regulations.
- Accede to WIPO and currently sourcing technical assistance in framing appropriate national legislation and enactment of laws;
- Local consultations on the establishment of an Intellectual property Organization;
- Has an established legal framework for the protection of intellectual property rights.

Table 6.3: Other PNG APEC commitments (continued)

Government procurement Short/medium/long term (1998 2020) • Continue to review its public procurement system within the National and provincial Government structure; Enhance transparency by making information available on specific requirements (if any); continue to develop clear guidelines on the system of government procurement.	• Has a liberal and decentralized Public Sector Procurement System for goods and services. The system encourages and promotes open tenders without discrimination to both local and foreign suppliers.
Services Business services: Short/medium/long term (1997-2020) • Identify new areas for privatization; • Review policies on service deregulation.	• Finish privatization of electricity, water supply, telecommunications and air services - will develop a program commencing in 1997 to corporatize and privatize services such as electricity (power generation, distribution & supply), air services. • Deregulate service sub-sectors subject to normal operational requirements (a) business – legal, architectural, engineering, computer, management and consulting (b) communication – courier, telecommunication, postal (c) construction and related engineering services – general construction work where limitation of national treatment is applied (d) banking and other financial services excluding insurance (e) tourism and travel-related services and (f) transport – maritime, passenger and freight transportation.

Source: PECC (1999)

APEC undertakings on government procurement are modest

APEC undertakings on government procurement are modest compared to the WTO plurilateral commitments. WTO arrangements are designed to improve the transparency of members' government procurement processes to limit the degree of discrimination against foreign suppliers. Unlike APEC undertakings, they require WTO members not to maintain price preferences in favour of domestic suppliers. For the sake of its economy PNG should therefore use its APEC involvement to ensure that government procurement arrangements do not, either intentionally or unintentionally, discriminate against more efficient foreign suppliers. Then it should re-consider its policy of not joining the WTO Government Procurement Agreement. The Solomon Islands and Fiji also would benefit from doing likewise.

Competition policy is being addressed in APEC, ahead of WTO

APEC members have also undertaken to enhance the competitive environment in the Asia Pacific region by introducing or maintaining effective and adequate competition policy and/or laws with associated enforcement policies. These are to be transparent so as to maximize the efficient operation of markets, and the competition among producers and traders, to the benefit of consumers. The WTO has no equivalent provisions concerning competition policy yet, but the desirability of doing so is currently being examined by WTO members.

PNG intends implementing a national competition policy

At present there is no national competition policy or specific competition legislation in PNG. The only laws protecting consumers from unfair trade practices are the Consumer Protection Act and the Price Control Act. However, the Government intends, over the longer term, to introduce a business practices act and a national competition policy. There is no specific competition law in Fiji or the Solomon Islands either.

Competition policy would be difficult to introduce well ...

However, implementing effective competition legislation and its enforcement is particularly resource-intensive and carries with it certain risks. There is no clear consensus among economists as to the best form for such policies to take. While the need for legislation prohibiting predatory pricing behaviour is widely accepted (although there are few documented cases of this actually happening), considerable disagreement exists as to the role competition policies should play in preventing anti-competitive behaviour.

... so open trade is the best competition policy for now

What is almost universally accepted is that open trade and import competition is the best means available for promoting competitive domestic markets for tradable products, particularly for developing countries with limited administrative capacity. In cases of non-traded services, the best competition policy is to deregulate and open up investment so that foreign-service suppliers can enter the domestic market as competitors.

7

Choosing the way forward

Pacific island economies are at the crossroads as globalization accelerates

PNG and the smaller Pacific island economies are at a major crossroads as we enter the third millennium. In the past decade or so the world has changed in very fundamental ways. The changes affect all economies, but especially those with policy regimes least suited to this fundamentally new environment. The creation of APEC in 1989, and more so the coming into being of the World Trade Organization in 1995 following the Uruguay Round, have contributed to the new environment. But they are less a cause of those fundamental changes than a response to them. It is the information technology revolution that is the main driver of this new wave of globalization. The abilities of national economies to adjust and take advantage of the opportunities offered by that phenomenon have differed greatly, but not so much because of different levels of economic development. Rather, it has been correlated with differences in the degree of openness of their economies, together with having appropriate institutions for good governance such as law and order and well-defined and enforced property rights.

The responses by other countries raise the stakes for Pacific island economies

The WTO agreements and the APEC process are crucial international institutional creations aimed at helping national governments respond to the forces of globalization. Key members are responding, and as a consequence globalization has accelerated — making it all the more imperative for other countries to adjust their policy regimes.

Globalization rewards good governance, but penalizes poor governance

A very positive feature of this phenomenon is that countries with good economic governance will be rewarded more in the future than they would have been in the past for their sensible policy stance. But the converse is also true. That is, countries with poor economic governance will be penalized more in the future than they would have been in the past. The most obvious manifestation of that penalty is the way in which foreign investments will be withdrawn and not replaced. A less obvious but probably more important manifestation will be a reduced ability of domestic firms to compete internationally, both at home and abroad.

The choice is therefore stark

Thus Pacific island countries face a stark choice: either they embrace globalization by adjusting their policy regimes to this new world, or their economies are destined to grow even slower. And they will grow slower not only relative to the rest of the world, but also in absolute terms as they fall further behind the technology leaders (given that technology transfer is closely related to openness of goods, services and capital markets).

WTO (and APEC) membership can assist policy reform

For PNG, Fiji and the Solomon Islands, their WTO membership has the potential to assist their governments adjust their policy regimes in appropriate ways. So too does the WTO accession process for those less-populous island economies that have already applied (Samoa, Tonga and Vanuatu). And by becoming a WTO Observer, the Forum Secretariat can assist the other Pacific island economies in learning the basic rules of good economic governance as it relates to trade, the essence of what GATT rules are about. The APEC process provides a supplementary avenue for learning about good governance. As an APEC member, PNG can acquire that directly; but FICs can get it indirectly through their close association not only with PNG but also with their other neighbours who are members.

Payoffs from reform are even higher now

The challenge for Pacific island governments and their citizens is before them. On the one hand, if they choose not to open up and reform their economies, their relatively poor economic growth and poverty alleviation performance of the past 25 years is likely not just to continue but to worsen. On the other hand, if they choose to embrace reform, the payoff will be even higher now than it would have been without this new wave of globalization. The payoff is greater now both because Pacific island economies are further behind than they were even just a few years ago, and because the opportunities for leapfrogging via technology transfer are so much greater now thanks to the information revolution.

Resistance to reform is still strong...

Embracing that challenge will not be easy politically or socially. Vested interests in the current protectionist trade regimes will fight to retain their privileged positions. Others will resent having to adjust to new ways of doing things. Most who would gain from reform are only vaguely aware of what could be in store for them, or not aware at all of the opportunities that could be before them. Hence, politicians with a short horizon will be reluctant to risk their positions by taking the lead.

... but to not reform would be very costly

Yet the 'status quo' option will become increasingly costly as globalization proceeds in the rest of the world. So how can Pacific island economies begin to respond?

Pacific island governments must build a constituency for reform

The most important priority for governments is to accept — and persuade their constituencies to accept — that trade, investment and other economic reforms are badly needed if private sector development and growth is to occur, since it is only by improving productivity that living standards can rise over the long term. Governments must be deeply committed to the process, and because that commitment has to be sustained it must be driven from a domestic base. While WTO (and APEC) membership can help reform-minded governments to implement market-opening measures, membership alone is insufficient for meaningful and sustainable reform.

Four domestic ingredients are needed:

At least four simultaneous domestic ingredients are needed at the outset if reform is to sustained: comprehensive awareness-raising campaigns; careful design of the reform program including the phasing of the implementation of each policy change; focused, socially productive adjustment assistance programs; and well-targeted technical and financial aid from abroad to help achieve the first three actions.

(i) raise awareness of opportunities, but also of the up-front adjustment costs

Communities, particularly in rural areas where the net benefits would be greatest, need to become much more acutely aware of the gains that could come their way if WTO-consistent market reforms were adopted. They also need to be aware that the gains would come gradually rather than all at once, whereas the costs of adjustment as reforms are implemented — even though they are one-off — will have to be borne up front. In the case of grossly distorted economies, the adjustment period could stretch out over a decade or more. If that is not understood at the outset, the risk is that disappointed expectations could lead to pressures for policy reversals. In extreme cases that could be worse than doing nothing, because it would involve double adjustment costs and no gains.

(ii) sequence the reforms and phase the implementation of the bigger ones

Prioritizing the reforms so they are appropriately sequenced and implemented at a pace that does not overwhelm the capacity of the legislature and the public administrators is obviously sensible. A key to keeping the costs of adjustment for the private sector manageable is to phase in the bigger reform programs over a pre-determined period that is announced at the outset. Thinking through the new policies before announcing them is crucial though, since subsequent changes to the new policies — or even just to the timing of the implementation phases — will reduce the credibility of the process and thereby discourage investors.

(iii) assist people's adjustment ...

Even though the benefits from market liberalization will far outweigh the up-front adjustment costs, the latter are both immediate and hit concentrated groups (e.g., those involved in industries that cannot compete when their protection from imports is reduced). Where reform-resistant interest groups are powerful politically, reform may only be possible if those affected are given an explicit adjustment incentive. In such cases, a special adjustment scheme may be needed, such as has been applied recently in Australia as part of the dairy market reforms. Such a scheme might be necessary in the extreme case of sugar reform in PNG's Ramu Valley.

... via better basic education in the long term ...

More generally, the best way the government can facilitate adjustment — which because of economic growth and globalization is happening to a considerable extent even when national policies are unchanged — is to equip people with the necessary skills for meeting the challenges and seizing the opportunities that change brings. All the international evidence points to better basic education being the key provider of such skills. Hence, some of the tax dividend from the faster economic growth that will result from reform could be used to improve the quantity and quality of primary and secondary education.

... and training programs for administrators in the short- to medium-term

Obviously, training programs for administrators and for trainers of administrators could enhance the capacity of the public service to facilitate adjustment to the reforms. One direct way of doing that at the outset is to provide trade and industry policy courses for bureaucrats and policy analysts. Both short courses in-country, and anything from one- to four-semester postgraduate programs in more advanced economies, have proved to be highly effective forms of capacity building for numerous developing countries in recent years following the Uruguay Round.

(iv) secure appropriate technical and financial aid

No Pacific island economy need confront these challenges alone. On the contrary, they can support each other by sharing ideas on how to design and implement reforms. Technical help is also available from the WTO Secretariat and member countries (provided to would-be as well as current WTO members) and from the World Bank and UNCTAD, financed by bilateral or multilateral aid flows. Such assistance is also available though the APEC process — for PNG at least — and from the South Pacific Forum

Secretariat. The necessary knowledge and goodwill exist in the international community to support the many aspects involved in comprehensive reform, should Pacific island countries choose to make them a long-term priority. Some countries, including PNG, have already taken some steps in the right direction.

The opportunity is there for leaders to embrace

The opportunity to embrace the reform process more comprehensively, and the rewards from doing so, have never been greater than they are now. It remains for leaders of Pacific islands to seize that opportunity.

APPENDICES

Appendix 1

Interviews held as part of the study

Date & time	Contact
6 June 2000	
0800	Mr Alan Mclay President Lae Chamber of Commerce & Industry
1000	Mr Wong Y Meng Chief Executive officer International Food Corporation
1430	Mr Kerry McDonough Managing Director Chemcare Pharmacy
1545	Mr Mark low Managing director Niugini Tablebirds
7 June 2000	
	Mr Michael Quenby Mr Steve Vaux General Manager Agricultural Manager Ramu Sugar Limited Ramu Sugar Limited
	Site inspection and group meeting with stakeholders from Ramu Sugar Limited and community representatives
8 June 2000	
0800	Mr Wayne Golding President Manufacturer's Council of PNG
1000	Dr Ben Imbun Department of Economics & Business Studies University of PNG

1100	Dr Agogo Mawuli
	National Research Institute
Date & time	Contact
1300	Mr Veali Vagi
	Prime Minister's Department
1400	Mr Thomas Abe
	Department of Trade & Industry
1500	Mr Evoa Lalatute
	Secretary
	Department of Foreign Affairs
9 June 2000	
Public Seminar on WTO and APEC	
12 June 2000	
0800	Mr Mike Manning
	Director
	Institute of National Affairs
0900	Mr Vincent Bull
	Managing Director
	BHP (PNG) Ltd
1000	Mr Rob Rudy
	Economic Advisor
	Internal Revenue Commission
1130	Mr Simon Peter
	Corporate Secretary
	Investment Promotion Authority
12 June 2000	
1330	Mr Wilson Kamit
	Governor
	Bank of PNG
1445	Dr Sam Lahis
	Project Coordinator
	Department of Agriculture & Livestock
1630	Mr David Conn
	President
	POM Chamber of Commerce & Industry

Appendix 2

Public Seminar on WTO & APEC

Granville Motel
9th June 2000

Session 1 Chairman
9.00-9.30 Introduction to WTO and APEC-Dr Samson Polume
9.30-9.45 Discussion and comments
9.45-10-15 The Government View-Michael Maue, Secretary, DTI

Session 2 Chairman: Samson Polume
10.15-10.30 Morning tea
10.30-11.00 Investment Promotion-Simon Peter, IPA
11.00-11-15 Discussion and comment
11.15-11.45 NGO Point of View- Lessons form Seattle-Lester Seri, Conservation Melanesia
11.45-12.0　Discussion

Session 3 Chairman
1.15-1.45 Union Point of View-John Paska
1.45-2.00 Discussion and comment
2.00-2.30 Manufacturers' Point of View-Manufacturers' Council
2.30-2.45 Discussion and comment

Session 4 Chairman: Mike Manning
2.45-3.00 Afternoon tea
3.00-3.30 Agricultural Point of View-RIC
3.30-3.45 Discussion and comment
3.45-4.15 Summary-Malcolm Bosworth, Consultant
4.15-5.00 General discussion and comment

Appendix 3

What WTO accession and membership involve

Participation in WTO will constitute the cornerstone for PNG trade policy development in the 21st century, as it will for those larger Pacific Island economies that have recently joined WTO (Fiji and Solomon Islands) or are in the process of joining (Samoa, Tonga and Vanuatu). In return for the rights and opportunities that membership of these clubs brings, there are also some obligations and challenges that must be faced. Governments sign on to those obligations presumably because they believe the benefits will outweigh the costs, even though some of the obligations offer political challenges in the short term. In particular, the process of negotiating accession to WTO consolidates and makes it more difficult to reverse a country's economic reforms.

Benefits and obligations of WTO membership

To become a WTO member is to join a club. Like all clubs, the WTO bestows benefits on members but there are some costs; it offers rights but with them come obligations; it provides new opportunities but also some challenges. Evidently the net benefits are overwhelmingly positive, given that more than 120 developing countries will be members within five years. But like all worthy clubs, there are rules to be followed, entry conditions to be met and formal accession procedures to follow. Occasionally the rules and obligations upset political sensitivities because some groups *within* a country may lose a privilege (e.g., protection from import competition), but almost invariably those rules boost the overall economy of each WTO member. The general benefits that come from the freer trade that those rules encourage include the following:

- better allocation of national resources towards industries with the strongest comparative advantage;

- enhanced learning and newer technologies from interacting more with the rest of the world;

- greater flexibility, via trade, for dealing with shock such as natural disasters;

- less wasteful rent-seeking lobbying activities by groups seeking government assistance and protection; and

- reduced poverty.

Three specific benefits of WTO membership are greater and more-secure market access abroad for a country's exports, access to a dispute resolution mechanism, and greater discipline at home in sound economic policy making.

On the first of these, WTO rules, and particularly GATT Articles I and III, ensure that a member's exporters are entitled to non-discriminatory treatment by other WTO members in terms of access to their markets. This involves two aspects. One is 'most-favoured-nation' (MFN) status, or the same market access as other WTO members, to any particular member's markets for most goods. The key exceptions at present involve farm products and textiles and clothing, which are subject to separate agreements involving some quantitative import restrictions still. But even with these goods, it may be possible for better (including faster-expanding) access to be negotiated bilaterally as part of acceding to the WTO. In general (again there are exceptions) an import tariff is the only measure that can be used to restrict market access. Moreover, that access is guaranteed through upper limits on those tariffs (called 'bindings'). Typically, members have made commitments not just to cap them but also to phase down over time many of those bound tariff rates, so their trading partner members can expect to enjoy an expansion over time in guaranteed access to such markets. The other non-discriminatory aspect is 'national treatment', which means that a country must treat foreign suppliers no less favourably than domestic suppliers.

Secondly, if a member feels another member is not playing by the rules, the WTO has a dispute settlement mechanism for resolving the issue. Thanks to the Uruguay Round, that mechanism is now much stronger, faster, impartial, and binding than was the case under the GATT prior to 1995. As a result, members are less inclined to bend or break WTO rules and, if they do, other members have a reasonable chance of bringing them back into line and/or being compensated. Again this brings much greater security of access to markets for WTO members as compared with non-members.

And thirdly, because WTO rules also apply to one's own policies, membership brings discipline to economic policymaking at home as well. This can be a major advantage for a government keen to provide sound economic governance but subject to interest-group pleading for special protectionist favours.

More specifically, members are required to tariffy their non-tariff import restrictions, bind them, and perhaps even agree to a phasing down in some of those bound rates over time (which reduces the risk of policy reversals); to free up trade in services over time, again with specific commitments recorded in its Schedules; to strengthen and enforce its intellectual property rights legislation; to reduce state support for or direction of other (especially trading) enterprises; to limit any domestic support for agricultural industries; and to enforce WTO rules uniformly and predictably. Typically, WTO members are more demanding in all these respects on acceding countries than on existing members, although perhaps less so for least-developed countries.

All trade and trade-related policy measures must be notified to the WTO Secretariat. This adds to domestic policy transparency, making it more difficult for interest groups to be protected without detection. Numerous WTO Agreements require a member to have a single enquiry point where WTO members can seek information on policies covered by those agreements (e.g., TBT, SPS, TRIPs and GATS). Members are also required to inform the WTO Secretariat each year if any significant policy changes occur, to provide statistical information annually in a set format, and to undertake with the Secretariat, probably every six years, a comprehensive review of the member's trade and trade-related policies and practices.

There are other notification requirements as well. For example, all state trading enterprises must be notified to the WTO's Council on Goods, even those enterprises not engaged in international trade. Any trade restrictions imposed or changed for balance-of-payments reasons, or for sanitary or phytosanitary reasons, must be reported to the WTO. Technical standards different from accepted international standards, and conformity assessment procedures, also have to be notified. So too do any trade-related investment measures and import licensing procedures that are not in conformity with Uruguay Round agreements, as do all subsidy programs and all GATT-inconsistent voluntary export restraints.

Clearly these notification and review requirements are non-trivial for the national government of a small developing economy, and require considerable cooperation and coordination among the relevant agencies of the various levels of government. Furthermore, an enquiry point must be created and maintained such that other WTO members can readily find up-to-date information about trade and trade-related policies. New trade practices and procedures must be codified into laws and regulations and recorded in an official journal to which other WTO members can have ready access.

An example of a problematic area relates to import licencing rules. All rules and procedures for obtaining import licences must be published, procedures must be simple and prompt, the licences in principle should be administered through a 'one-stop shop' (or at most two), applicants have the right to ask for an explanation of non-approval and to appeal the decision, and a great deal of statistical information must be made available.

The steps to WTO accession

There is a series of steps required before a country can accede to the WTO. In the course of taking these steps, a country gradually amends its policies and institutions in readiness to abide by WTO rules and accept the obligations of membership.

The first step (although it is not obligatory) is to request Observer status so that national government officials can begin learning from the inside as to how the WTO institution works. When ready, the country submits a letter of application that triggers the establishment of a Working Party to examine the applicant's trade policies and practices, to organise accession negotiations, and to prepare the Protocol of Accession.

The next big step towards WTO accession is to prepare a Memorandum on the country's foreign trade regime. For a country in which policy transparency is not the norm, this is a major undertaking. Background information on the economy and domestic economic policies, detailed statistics on the country's foreign trade and investment, an outline of its legislative and bureaucratic frameworks for making and enforcing policies affecting foreign trade, and a copy of all the laws and regulations are required. In addition, the Memorandum must detail every current and agreed future policy measure affecting trade in goods, foreign investment policy and regulations, the trade-related intellectual property regime, the trade-related services regime, and any bilateral or plurilateral trade or economic integration agreements to which the country is a signatory. And a comprehensive tariff schedule in the detailed harmonized system nomenclature must be attached.

This Memorandum is circulated to all WTO members who are invited to submit in writing any questions of clarification. Once the country has compiled its answers to these questions, they are submitted to the Working Party, which triggers a series of review sessions. The frequency and length of meetings and the overall time this step takes depend heavily on the speed and comprehensiveness of the accedent's responses to the initial and follow-up questions: this step in principle could be completed in just a few months, but in practice (as in China's case) it could take several years.

Once the examination of the country's foreign trade regime is sufficiently advanced, members initiate bilateral market access negotiations on goods and services and on the other terms to be agreed. Even then, further fact-finding work on the trade regime may continue in parallel with those negotiations. Negotiations also proceed on a multilateral basis through the Working Party, during which three draft schedules of commitments have to be prepared. They relate to: tariffs (to be reduced and bound or subjected to ceiling bindings) and other measures affecting trade in goods; market access, domestic support and export subsidies affecting agricultural trade (which again have to be bound); and services trade commitments. They may specify phase-in periods and allow temporary maintenance of current practices for a limited period.

In practice these market access commitments are negotiated with one or more of the WTO members who are principal suppliers, but they are extended on an unconditional MFN basis to all WTO members. The commitments may extend beyond the scope of the Uruguay Round agreements (e.g., privatization). In this process the acceding country cannot seek 'concessions' from members, but on accession it will have the guarantee of MFN access to all members' markets (something which it may have been denied previously).

Once the negotiations on the three schedules of commitments are concluded, the Working Party will submit its report together with a draft Decision and Protocol of Accession to the General Council or Ministerial Conference of the WTO. Acceptance requires two-thirds of WTO members to approve it.

Special and differential treatment for developing and least-developed countries

In addition to receiving the standard WTO membership benefits such as MFN and national treatment, the right to some of the low-tariff rate quota access to others' agricultural markets, the possibility of accelerated growth in access to US and EU markets for textiles and clothing, and access to the WTO's Dispute Settlement Body, those WTO members that are developing countries, and in particular least-developed economies including those in transition from central planning, also receive some special (although typically temporary) treatment in the WTO. This crops up in many places in the WTO agreements. However, this is not a set of rights automatically given in full to an acceding country. On the contrary, each of those items must be negotiated, and in practice many developing and transition countries (most notably China) find it difficult to secure much in the way of special and differential treatment even as developing countries let alone as least-developed.

Appendix 4

Determinants of structural change in a developing economy

One of the most striking features of economic development is the relative decline of the primary sector in growing economies. Also typical, particularly of densely populated countries, is a decline in their agricultural comparative advantage as industrialization proceeds. Whether that leads to declines in food self-sufficiency and the value of net imports of agricultural products are moot points: it depends in part on policy trends, which happen often to gradually change from disfavouring to favouring agriculture relative to other tradable sectors over the long term. This Appendix seeks to explain these trends.

Why the primary sector declines relatively as an economy grows

A primitive economy with few trading opportunities necessarily has to devote most of its resources to the provision of food. Agriculture's shares of national output and employment therefore start at high levels. As economic development proceeds, however, agriculture's shares of GDP and employment typically fall. This has commonly been attributed to two phenomena: the slow rise in the demand for food as compared with other goods and services as incomes rise (that is, relatively low price and income elasticities of demand); and the more rapid development (at least historically – see Martin and Mitra 1998) of new technologies for primary sectors, relative to those for other sectors, which leads to expanding food supplies per hectare and per worker. Some of those new technologies can be imported by a late-developing economy from those more-advanced economies that were similarly endowed in earlier decades with a scarcity (or abundance) of land per worker, and then adapted relatively easily to local conditions. Together those forces suggest we should expect a decline in agriculture's terms of trade in international markets, and more so the stronger is productivity growth in agriculture compared with other sectors.

In practise that decline in the terms of trade for primary product exporters is exacerbated by the gradual policy change, from taxing to subsidising agriculture, that so often accompanies the economic development of nations (Anderson 1994, 1995a). The weight of empirical evidence seems consistent with that expectation, in that agricultural prices appear to have declined considerably relative to industrial product prices during the past century, even after adjusting prices of (particularly non-farm) products for changes in quality (Grilli and Yang 1988).

But what about in an open agrarian economy that can trade all of its products internationally at those terms of trade? If such an economy opened itself fully to international trade, the importance of agriculture would increase and the country would export agricultural produce and with the foreign exchange proceeds would import other products. If productivity growth and/or factor accumulation occurred in this open economy and the international terms of trade remained unchanged, agriculture's share of national product would rise or fall depending on whether that productivity growth was biased toward farm or non-farm production. If that growth was sectorally unbiased, agriculture's share would remain unchanged. However, if economic growth is occurring abroad and so altering relative prices internationally, the agricultural sector of a small open economy would decline unless the economy's own growth is biased towards agriculture sufficiently for the quantity changes to more than offset the adverse change in the terms of trade that result from global economic growth.

The above assumes all products are tradable internationally. In reality, however, a large part of a developing economy involves the production and consumption of nontradable goods and services. These are items for which the costs of overcoming barriers to trading internationally -- especially transport costs -- are prohibitively expensive. The price of nontradables is determined by domestic demand and supply conditions because, unlike tradables, in equilibrium the quantity of nontradables demanded has to equal the quantity supplied domestically. Since the vast majority of nontradables are services, and since the income elasticity of demand for services tends to be well above unity, the demand for nontradables as a group is likely to be income elastic.

To see how taking into account the existence of nontradables alters the above conclusions, think of the two tradable sectors as comprising one super-sector of tradables and the rest of the economy as comprising nontradables whose demand is income elastic (which means the demand for tradables as a group must be income inelastic for their weighted average to sum to unity). Then if both sectors enjoyed equally rapid productivity growth, the demand conditions would ensure that the GDP share of tradables declines with economic growth. And if, for the reasons mentioned above, agriculture's importance is likely to decline within the tradables super-sector, it is even more likely to decline in relative importance in the total economy. Thus even for an open economy with an exceptionally dynamic farm sector, retaining resources in agriculture over the long term is unlikely; in fact, they will tend to be retained only in economies that are accumulating/importing non-farm resources relatively slowly and/or are suffering very slow productivity growth in their non-agricultural sectors, ceteris paribus (Anderson 1987).

The above reasoning is sufficient also for explaining the decline in agriculture's share of employment unless labour productivity is much slower in agriculture than in other sectors. Official data imply that agriculture's share of employment has not been declining as rapidly as the GDP share in growing economies.37 The latter should not be seen as a sign of relative deterioration in labour productivity in the agricultural sector, however, as more care is needed in measuring farm labour input. Specifically, the proportion of farm household labour time spent in non-farm activities needs to be counted as agricultural only as much as the output is attributed to the agricultural sector. Typically in practice the recording of output is changed faster than the recording of employment and so the decline in agriculture's share of employment tends to be understated more in national accounts than the decline in the GDP share.

This decline in agriculture's GDP share results partly because post-farm gate activities, such as taking produce to market, get commercialized and taken over by specialists in the service sector. In such cases the farmers receive a lower price, in return for which their households spend less time going to market. Another contributing factor is that previous manual farm jobs such as spreading manure and weeding crops disappear as farm chemicals become more profitable, available and affordable with higher-yielding crop varieties, the seeds for which also have to be purchased in the case of hybrid varieties. As a result, value added by the farm household's own labour, land and capital, as a share of the gross value of agricultural output, falls over time as purchased intermediate inputs become more important. In fact, Anderson (1987, Table 2.1) provides evidence showing that the value-added share typically falls much more for agriculture than for the industrial sector. This increasing use of purchased intermediate inputs and off-farm services by farmers adds to the relative decline of the farm sector per se in overall GDP and employment.

---

[37] For low-income countries the share of agriculture in GDP fell from 34 to 25 per cent between 1980 and 1995, while the share of the labour force in agriculture as measured declined only slightly (from 73 to 69 per cent between 1980 and 1990 – World Bank 1997a).

One might also expect agriculture's share of exports to decline with economic growth, although with less certainty than for agriculture's shares of GDP and employment. To see this, consider again an open economy in a world in which the international price of agricultural relative to other goods is declining over time because of economic growth abroad. If this open economy is growing and if its output growth is insufficiently biased towards the non-farm sectors to match the non-farm bias in domestic demand growth, agriculture's share of exports may not decline: excess supply may grow more rapidly for farm than for non-farm products. But if this economy is not growing or its growth is concentrated in non-farm sectors, agriculture's share of its exports would decline, in part at least because of the decline in the relative price of farm products internationally.

Why agricultural self sufficiency may or may not decline with growth

What determines whether a country is a net agricultural exporter or importer at a point in time? And how will that position change over time? A nation's self sufficiency in farm products depends largely on its relative factor endowments compared with the rest of the world's (the key determinant of agricultural comparative advantage) as well as on government policies at home and abroad. Leaving the latter aside for the moment, how can we conceptualize the impact of the former on a country's trade composition?

The role of relative factor endowments

Perhaps the most appropriate simple model for explaining comparative advantage in a growth setting is that developed by Krueger (1977) and explored further by Deardorff (1984a). It is a model of two tradable sectors each using intersectorally mobile labour plus one specific factor (natural resource capital or produced capital). Assuming labour exhibits diminishing marginal product in each sector (and assuming for the moment that there are no services or nontradables, and no policy distortions), then at a given set of international prices the real wage is determined by the overall per worker endowment of both forms of capital. The commodity composition of a country's trade -- that is, the extent to which a country is a net exporter of primary or industrial products -- is determined by its endowment of natural resource capital (farmland, forests, fisheries and minerals) relative to industrial capital *compared with that ratio for the rest of the world*. Within the primary sector, the more abundant a country's per worker endowment of forests and minerals compared with arable land and industrial capital, the stronger will be its comparative advantage in primary products other than food crops. That is important for understanding changes in comparative advantage over time. For example, a minerals or energy raw materials discovery, or an increase in the international price of minerals or energy, would strengthen the country's comparative advantage in mining and weaken its comparative advantage in farm and other goods, ceteris paribus. It would also encourage mobile resources to move into the production of nontradables as their demand strengthened and prices rose, further reducing farm and industrial production.[38] On the other hand, net deforestation simultaneously depletes the stock of trees and natural forest land and increases the potential area of land for agriculture, thereby eventually strengthening the country's comparative advantage in agriculture as a whole, ceteris paribus.

Of course domestic or foreign savings can be invested to enhance the stock and/or improve the quality not only of industrial capital but also of labour or natural resources, in addition to providing capital specific to the nontradables

---

[38] (Corden 1984). In fact the increased demand for nontradables (and other products) would begin as soon as expectations about future income prospects rose, which could be well before the export boom shows up in the trade statistics in the case where the exports are preceded by FDI inflows for investments with a long lead time (Corden 1982).

sector. Any such increase in the net stock of produced capital per worker will put upward pressure on real wages. That will encourage, in all sectors, the use of more labour-saving techniques and the development and/or importation of new technologies that are less labour intensive. Which type of capital would expand fastest in a free-market setting depends on their expected rates of return. The more densely populated, natural resource-poor a country, the greater the likelihood that the highest payoff would be in expanding its capital stocks for non-primary sectors. At early stages of development of such a country with a relatively small stock of natural resources per worker, wages would be very low and the country would have a comparative cost advantage in unskilled labour-intensive, standard-technology manufactures. Then as the stock of industrial capital grows, there would be a gradual move toward exporting more capital- and skill-intensive manufactures. Natural resource-abundant countries, on the other hand, would enter manufacturing at a later stage of development. Such countries are likely to have remained more than fully self sufficient in agricultural products for longer (although less so the greater their comparative advantage in minerals or other primary products, ceteris paribus), and their first industrial exports would be comparatively capital intensive. [39]

---

[39] Notwithstanding its popular media coverage, the theory of 'competitive' advantage espowsed by Porter (1990) does not supersede this theory of comparative advantage based on relative factor endowments. Warr (1994) explains why, noting that the confusion arises because while both are concerned with international competitiveness in a global context, the former applies to firms within an industry or sector (which focus on their private costs and benefits alone) whereas the latter is concerned with the competitiveness of industries and sectors from a national viewpoint, taking account of all (including social) costs and benefits. The theory of comparative advantage in its simplest form is based on numerous assumptions which, as critics never tire to point out, are unrealistic. However, the basic thrust of the theory survives when these assumptions are relaxed and the theory is made dynamic, and strong empirical support from a wide range of countries can be found for the theory.

What determines the extent to which a country's agricultural exports will be unprocessed rather than processed products, low quality rather than high quality, and non-perishable rather than perishable? The capital intensity of production of the latter will play some part, but most of the explanation will have to do with the cost/speed of in-country transportation and communications, with packing, grading and storage facilities, with sea and air port facilities, and with the volume of domestic urban sales of processed, high-quality and perishable products. The latter sales volume is important because it provides the derived demands for processing and distribution services which, when sufficiently large, allow economies of scale to lower the price at which the more sophisticated products can be made available for export).

The role of policies affecting agricultural incentives

The above expectations about agricultural self-sufficiency drawn from the theory of comparative advantage are based on the assumption of no interference in markets by governments. But in fact most countries intervene in markets and alter incentives facing producers and consumers.

From a national viewpoint, four levels of intervention can be distinguished. One is intervention abroad that alters a country's terms of trade. Another is intervention at the national macro level to encourage savings and investment: the provision of price stability (i.e., low inflation), responsible fiscal policies, the optimal regulation of an open financial market, law and order including for the establishment and protection of property rights, the optimal provision and geographic distribution of public goods such as infrastructure, and the offsetting of externalities (which again could involve sectoral or geographic biases). The third level of intervention has to do with the biasing of prices in favour of non-tradables via an overvalued currency (or, less commonly, in favour of tradables via undervaluing the nation's currency). And the fourth level of intervention has to do with altering output and input prices within the grouping of tradables sectors so that some tradables sectors enjoy more effective assistance from the government than others.[40]

The fact that sub-optimal intervention is rampant would make it difficult to qualify the above conclusions from comparative cost theory, were it not for the fact that governments intervene in a fairly consistent fashion. Five empirical features of intervention are worth mentioning. First, policies in high-income countries tend to overprice farm relative to nonfarm products while policies in lower-income countries tend to underprice them. Second, the degree of overpricing (underpricing) is highly positively correlated with the degree of agricultural comparative disadvantage (advantage). Third, over time countries tend to gradually change their policy induced distortion pattern away from negatively to positively assisting farmers and from effectively subsidizing to hurting food consumers. Fourth, much of the disincentive to agriculture in developing countries comes not from *direct* underpricing but *indirectly* via manufacturing protection and overvaluation of the nation's currency. And fifth, most national governments have an urban bias in their provision of public infrastructure (transport, communications, etc.) and human capital (education, health, information production and dissemination, etc.) which decreases but rarely reverses with economic development, especially when the quality of those investments is properly accounted for. These transitions tend to occur at a faster rate the faster an economy is growing and, in the case of relative price distortions, to reach the point of intersectoral policy neutrality at an earlier stage of economic development the weaker a country's agricultural comparative advantage (Anderson 1995a).

---

[40] As Corden (1994, Ch, 15) makes clear, these levels are useful in sorting out the different uses people make of the term "international competitiveness", which could apply to all sectors, to just the grouping of sectors producing tradables, or to just one or a subset of those tradables sectors.

According to one recent set of estimates, the net effect on international prices of temperate foods of this relative overpricing in rich countries is almost exactly offset by the underpricing of those products in poorer countries (Tyers and Anderson 1992, Ch. 6). But that is less likely to be the case for edible oils, and it would certainly not be the case for beverages and other tropical products not produced in high-income countries: in both of these latter cases, the underpricing domestically in developing countries dominates, causing international prices for these products to be higher than they would be under global free trade.

Three important consequences follow from these facts. One is that countries are trading less in farm products than would be the case without intervention: countries with a comparative advantage in farming tend to be exporting less, and those with a comparative disadvantage in farming tend to be importing less (and may even be depressing international prices further by using export subsidies to dispose of protection-induced surpluses, as in Western Europe). Another is that the relative price of agricultural products in international markets has been under even greater pressure to decline in the course of global economic growth than suggested in the discussion above, as more and more upper middle-income developing countries gradually move away from taxing to subsidizing farmers. And the third consequence of these facts is that it has left ample scope to reform policies affecting farmer and consumer incentives, the effects of which will depend heavily on the pace and nature of multilateral, regional and unilateral reforms in the various commodity markets. It is conceivable, for example, that an increase in net farm imports by high-income countries following the Uruguay Round and its successor could coincide with an increase in net exports of agricultural products from developing countries undertaking unilateral reforms. That would have offsetting effects on international farm prices but reinforcing effects on quantities traded as both sets of countries better exploit their respective comparative advantages. And it is expected that the discipline placed on developing and transition economies (including those

subsequently acceding to the WTO) by the Uruguay Round
Agreement on Agriculture not to raise farm producer or
export subsidies will, in the long run at least as bound
agricultural tariffs are lowered, reduce the likelihood that
agricultural disincentives are replaced by protectionist
policies in the future.

The role of policies affecting manufactures

The trade policy bias in favour of import-substituting
industrialization, discussed above, has a similar effect on
unskilled labour-intensive manufacturing in a newly
industrializing economy as it does on agriculture. Limiting
imports through protectionism reduces the demand for
foreign currency and thereby causes the real exchange rate
to appreciate. That effectively holds back the development
of *all* industries otherwise able to export,[41] including those
light ones in which a poor country's manufacturing
comparative advantage will first emerge. They are the very
industries most likely to benefit from relocating or
establishing in rural areas to take advantage of lower
wages and other costs of production there. Hence not only
agriculture but also rural industrialization is hampered by
all-too-common   protectionist   import-substituting
industrial policies.

The role of rural infrastructure investments

Needless to say, the move from subsistence-only farm
production to having a marketable surplus of food, and the
emergence of cash cropping, depend on the provision of
rural roads, radio, post and telecoms to lower the cost of
transport, information and communication for rural
people. Constructing those infrastructures and maintaining
them provide off-farm work for farm households, but more
importantly those infrastructures spawn additional new
service-sector jobs in rural areas and elsewhere for
transporting,   grading,   processing,   packing,   and

---

[41] For more on how protection against imports effectively taxes
exports, see Clements and Sjaastad (1984).

distributing the marketed farm products. The opening up or extending of rural roads and communications also expand the effective demand for purchased farm inputs such as improved seed varieties, chemical ferrtilizers, pesticides, farm machinery, and fuel.

Rural roads, electricity and telecommunications also make rural industrialization more profitable for unskilled labour-intensive industries not connected to primary sectors. True, those roads also make it easier for rural workers to drift to urban areas, which would close the urban-rural wage gap somewhat. But many workers will stay put because for much of the year they are fully occupied in seasonal farm work. The more that rural industrialization is successful, the more the country's comparative advantage would move away from the primary sectors. The new jobs created by those off-farm activities have been shown to contribute substantially not only to economic growth but also to reducing absolute poverty and rural-income inequality in many modernising agrarian economies. They also slow the growth of urban pollution and congestion.

All of this suggests a high social rate of return to investments in rural infrastructure, and more so the less government price and trade policies discriminate between primary and manufacturing sectors. The returns would be higher the freer the economy is of government interventions. This is because in the presence of protection manufacturers sell mainly to domestic consumers and buy inputs from other producers. Those linkages encourage a concentration of manufacturing in the cities. By contrast, in an open economy most sales of domestically produced manufactures are exports and many inputs are imported, so together with higher urban property prices those factors can eventually encourage rural industrialization (Krugman 1998). This new theory of economic geography suggests a government can slow or reverse the growth of large urban cities by freeing trade and boosting rural infrastructure.

Empirical evidence

Time series evidence provides strong empirical support for the comparative advantage theory outlined above, notwithstanding policy distortions. The time series evidence for Asia's less developed economies is clear from the middle columns of Table A4.1. The first four columns of that table summarize the relative resource endowments and economic growth rates of Asia's economies. Leaving aside the centrally planned economies of Indo-China and North Korea, three groups of developing economies are identifiable: the NIEs of South Korea and Taiwan, the large ASEAN economies plus China, and the South Asian economies. The first are extremely densely populated, very rapidly growing and with high incomes; the second are moderately densely populated, rapidly growing (the Philippines only in the 1990s) and with moderate incomes; and the third are very densely populated, slowly growing prior to the 1990s and with low incomes. Theory would lead us to expect the first group to have a weak and rapidly declining comparative advantage in agriculture, the second to have a stronger agricultural comparative advantage at the same per capita income but one that is nonetheless declining, and the third to have an in-between and only slowly declining comparative advantage in farm products.

The final four columns of Table A4.1 support that theory. They show the trends in two indicators of agricultural trade specialization. One is the so-called 'revealed' comparative advantage index, defined as agriculture's share of a country's merchandise exports relative to agriculture's share of global merchandise exports. The other is agricultural exports minus imports as a ratio of agricultural exports plus imports. The latter therefore takes a value between minus and plus one, and is zero when a country is 100 per cent self sufficient in farm products.

Table A4.1: Agriculture's shares of GDP and merchandise exports and trade specialization indexes, various Asian countries, 1965 to 1995

	Land & GNP/worker (1995, % of world av.)			GNP/capita growth (% pa)	Share of GDP from agric. (%)		Agriculture's share of merchandise exports (%)		Agric. comparative advantage index[a]		Agric. net export index[b]	
	Arable Land	Total land	GNP	1970-1995	1970	1995	1965-69	1993-95	1965-69	1993-95	1965-69	1993-95
Japan	12	12	750	3.2	6	2	2	1	0.08	0.05	-0.89	-0.74
South Korea	18	10	210	10.0	26	7	12	1	0.60	0.15	-0.67	-0.71
North Korea	32	21	<25	na	Na	na	11	7	0.58	0.77	-0.26	-0.70
Taiwan	18	8	290	7.0	16	3	39	4	1.96	0.45	0.20	-0.30
Indonesia	65	43	22	4.7	45	17	53	11	2.69	1.28	0.54	0.16
Malaysia	180	87	106	4.0	29	13	46	11	2.35	1.24	0.34	0.33
Philippines	62	22	26	0.6	30	22	49	11	2.51	1.26	0.45	-0.10
Thailand	115	32	48	5.2	26	11	76	16	3.87	1.80	0.68	0.50
China	25	27	7	6.9	35	21	40	6	2.08	0.72	0.19	0.04
Cambodia	147	75	6	Na	Na	51	95	na	4.88	na	0.80	na
Laos	72	205	7	Na	Na	52	14	22	0.70	2.50	-0.95	0.36
Myanmar	79	59	<7	1.2	Na	63	71	43	3.63	4.89	0.68	-0.01
Vietnam	36	19	5	Na	Na	28	20	27	1.06	2.99	-0.77	0.40
Bangladesh	29	4	5	1.5	55	31	45	5	2.29	0.53	0.13	-0.74
India	76	15	8	2.4	45	29	36	14	1.85	1.58	-0.22	0.37
Nepal	44	29	4	1.3	67	42	84[c]	17	5.53[c]	1.91	0.78	-0.44
Pakistan	88	35	8	2.9	37	26	74	12	3.75	1.32	0.08	-0.36
Sri Lanka	41	16	15	3.2	28	23	96	15	4.91	1.66	0.37	-0.02
WORLD	100	100	100	1.4	8	5	20	9	1.00	1.00	0.00	0.00

[a] Agriculture's share of the country's exports relative to agriculture's share of global merchandise exports.

[b] Agricultural exports minus imports as a ratio of agricultural exports plus imports.

[c] 1975-79.

Sources: World Bank (1997a) and FAO (1997).

Appendix 5

List of trade policy terms

Binding commitments (services)
Binding (sometimes bound) commitments are a legal obligation not to make market access conditions more restrictive than described in a country's schedule of commitments. They are enforceable and may only be breached through negotiation with affected trading partners. A country breaching a binding may have to offer compensation.

Bindings (goods)
A binding (also called concession) is a legal obligation not to raise tariffs on particular products above the specified rate agreed in GATT negotiations and incorporated in a country's schedule of concessions. Bindings are enforceable through the GATT. Their purpose is to provide greater commercial certainty through a ceiling which cannot be breached.

Commercial presence
Any type of business or professional establishment within the territory of a GATS member for the purpose of supplying a service. This includes juridical persons, branches and representative offices.

Copyright
The exclusive right to do certain things with an original work, including the right to reproduce, publish, perform the work in public and to make adaptations of it.

Council for Trade in Goods
The body administering 13 agreements covering trade in goods. The most important of these is the GATT.

Council for Trade in Services	The body administering the General Agreement on Trade in Services.
Council for TRIPS	The body administering the Agreement on Trade-Related Aspects of Intellectual Property Rights. Its role is to monitor the operation of the agreement and members' compliance with it.
Countervailing measures	Special duties imposed on imports to offset the benefits of subsidies to producers or exporters in the exporting country. GATT Article VI and the Agreement on Subsidies and Countervailing Measures set out the rules for imposing such measures.
Dispute settlement	Resolution of conflict, usually through a compromise between opposing claims, sometimes through an intermediary. Procedures for dispute resolution are set out in articles XXII and XXIII of the GATT, articles XXII and XXIII of the GATS and article 64 of TRIPS. All of these agreements follow the unified procedures set out by the WTO.
Export quotas	Restrictions or ceilings imposed by an exporting country on the value or volume of certain products. They are designed to protect domestic producers and consumers from temporary shortages of these products or to improve their prices on world markets.
Financial services	Banking, general insurance, life insurance, funds management, securities trading and advisory services related to these activities.
Free trade area	A group of two or more countries that have eliminated tariff and most non-tariff barriers affecting trade among themselves. Participating countries may continue to apply their own tariffs on external goods, or they may agree on a

	common external tariff.
GATS	General Agreement on Trade in Services
GATT	General Agreement on Tariffs and Trade
General Council	This is a body composed of all WTO members. It has general authority to supervise the various agreements under the jurisdiction of the WTO.
Geneva Convention	Protects a producer of phonograms against the making of duplicates without his or her consent. The convention currently has 52 members.
Horizontal commitments	Horizontal commitments apply to all services trade covered in a schedule of commitments. Generally, they relate to investment, formation of corporate structures, land acquisition, the movement of personnel, etc.
Import quotas	Restrictions or ceilings imposed by an importing country on the value or volume of certain products. They are designed to protect domestic producers from the effects of lower-priced imported products.
Industrial property	Mainly deals with inventions, trade marks and industrial designs, but also the repression of unfair competition.
Intellectual property	The rights of creators in the industrial, scientific, technological, musical and artistic fields. Rights relate to patents, trademarks, industrial designs, layout designs of integrated circuits, copyright, geographical indications and confidential information (trade secrets).
Juridical person	A legal entity, such as a corporation, trust, partnership, joint venture, sole proprietorship, association, etc., formed for the purpose of supplying a service.
MFN (goods)	Most-favoured-nation treatment: all GATT contracting parties grant each other treatment as

favourable as they give to any other country in the application and administration of customs regulations, tariffs and related charges.

MFN (intellectual property)   Most-favoured-nation treatment: the obligation to treat intellectual property right holders from all TRIPS members in the same way, subject to some exceptions under article 4 of TRIPS.

MFN (services)   Most-favoured-nation treatment: the obligation to treat service providers from all GATS member countries and their services equally. MFN does not imply a qualitative standard.

MFN exemptions (services)   In services trade, permission granted to a member country not to apply MFN treatment in a given sector. MFN exemptions are for a maximum of 10 years, and they have to be reviewed after 5 years.

Modes of delivery for services   Services can be delivered in four ways:

1. *cross-border supply*, where the producer remains in one territory and the consumer in another;

2. *consumption abroad*, where the consumer travels from one country to the country of the service producer to obtain the service;

3. *commercial presence*, where services are provided through establishment in the other country; and

4. *presence of natural persons*, where the producer travels from one country to another to produce or deliver a service.

Multilateral trade negotiations   Multilateral trade negotiations (also known as *rounds*) aim to reach mutually beneficial agreements reducing barriers to world trade. Eight such rounds have been held under GATT auspices since 1947. Each round has consisted of long bargaining sessions.

National treatment (goods)	Non-discrimination in domestic regulations and requirements, including taxation, between like domestic and imported goods.
National treatment (intellectual property)	A member of TRIPS must accord to the nationals of other members treatment no less favourable that it accords to its own nationals, but there may be some exceptions to this because of rights under the Paris, Berne or Rome Conventions and the Treaty on Integrated Circuits.
National treatment (services)	The obligation to guarantee foreign service provides and their services equivalent treatment to domestic service providers.
Natural persons	Persons who are citizens or permanent residents of a GATS member country. If they are service suppliers, they have rights under the GATS.
Negative listings	Used in the schedules of commitments under the GATS. Negative listing means that all service activities are covered by all provisions of the GATS unless they are listed as subject to some limitations on market access and national treatment. The advantage of this method is that all new services are automatically covered. Developed countries have used this method for the financial services commitments.
Non-tariff measures	Government measures other than tariffs that restrict imports. Examples include quantitative restrictions, import licensing, voluntary restraint arrangements and variable levies. For the purposes of the Uruguay Round, non-tariff measures also included domestic support arrangements that distort or impede trade, such as price support programs and production subsidies.
Patent	The right given to inventors to exclude others

for a specified period from making, using or
selling a new, useful, non-obvious invention.

Patent — Provides for the filing of an *international* patent
Cooperation — application in member states. Has the same
Treaty — effect in member states as filing an application
with a national patent office.

Positive — Countries may inscribe their commitments
listings — under the GATS in the form of positive listings.
In this way, only listed activities are subject to all
GATS disciplines. The disadvantage is that all
services have to be listed even if there are no
market access or national treatment limitations.
Most countries activities have made their listings
in this form.

Quantitative — Limits or quotas on the amounts of particular
restrictions — commodities that can be imported or exported
during a given period. They are usually
measured by volume, but sometimes by value.

Reciprocity — The practice by which governments extend
similar concessions to each other, as when one
government lowers tariffs or other barriers
impeding imports in exchange for equivalent
concessions from a trading partner. This is also
known as a *balance of concessions*. Concessions
made as a result of reciprocal bargaining must
be extended on an MFN-basis to all GATT or
GATS members.

Retaliation — Action taken by a country to restrain imports
from a country that has increased a tariff or
imposed other measures adversely affecting its
exports.

Schedules of — Schedules of commitment are a key requirement
commitments — and component under the GATS. They perform
a function similar to the tariff schedules for
goods under the GATT. Schedules allow service

	exporters to examine the extent to which they have guaranteed access to markets.
Sectoral commitments	Entries covering specific service sectors or sub-sectors in the schedules of commitments. Examples are accountancy, freight-forwarding or life insurance. A sectoral commitment attracts a higher level of GATS rights and obligations. A commitment may not be made more restrictive for at least three years.
Special and differential treatment	The concept that exports of developing countries should be given preferential access to markets of developed countries, and that developing countries participating in trade negotiations need not reciprocate fully the concessions they receive.
Tariff	A duty (or tax) levied on goods going from customs area to another. Tariffs raise the price of imported goods and make them less competitive in the market of the importing country.
Tariff quota	The application of a reduced tariff rate for a specified quantity of imported goods.
Trademarks	Words, names, symbols, devices or combinations of these, used by manufacturers and merchants to identify their goods and to distinguish them from others.
Unbound commitments	Unbound commitments give the listing country complete flexibility to change its trading regime in the affected activity without the need to offer compensation. Unbound commitments are therefore much less valuable than bound commitments.

Source: Goode (1998).

References

Anderson, K. (1987), 'On Why Agriculture Declines With Economic Growth', *Agricultural Economics* 1(3): 195-207, June.

Anderson, K. (1994), 'Food Price Policy in East Asia', *Asian-Pacific Economic Literature* 8(2): 15-30, November.

Anderson, K. (1995), 'Lobbying Incentives and the Pattern of Protection in Rich and Poor Countries', *Economic Development and Cultural Change* 43(2): 401-23, January.

Anderson, K. (1998), 'Are Resource-Abundant Economies Disadvantaged?' *Australian Journal of Agricultural and Resource Economics* 42(1): 1-23, March.

AusAID (1999), *The Economy of Papua New Guinea, Macroeconomic Policies: Implications for Growth and Development in the Informal Sector*, Australian Agency for International Development, Canberra.

Ben-David, D., H. Nordstrom and L.A. Winters (1999), *Trade, Income Disparity and Poverty*, Special Study 5, World Trade Organization, Geneva.

CIE (1997), *Gaining from Gas; the economic contribution of the Papua New Guinea LNG project*, Centre for International Economics, Canberra.

Clements, K.W. and L.A. Sjaastad (1984), *How Protection Taxes Exports*, Thames Essay No. 39, Trade Policy Research Centre, London.

Commonwealth Secretariat/World Bank (2000), *Small States: Meeting Challenges in the Global Economy*, World Bank, Washington, D.C., April. (Downloadable at www.worldbank.org/html/extdr/smallstates)

Corden, W.M. (1982), 'Exchange Rate Policy and the Resources Boom', *Economic Record* 58(160): 18-31, March.

Corden, W.M. (1984), 'Booming Sector and Dutch Disease Economics: Survey and Consolidation', *Oxford Economic Papers* 36(3): 359-80, November.

Corden, W.M. (1994), *Economic Policy, Exchange Rates and the International System*, University of Chicago Press, Chicago.

Corden, W.M. (1997a), *Trade Policy and Economic Welfare* (second edition), Clarendon Press, Oxford.

Corden, W.M. (1997b), 'Tell Us Where the New Jobs Will Come From', Ch. 7 in his collection on *The Road to Reform: Essays in Australian Economic Policy*, Addison Wesley, Sydney.

Dollar, D. (1992), 'Outward-Oriented Developing Economies Really Do Grow More Rapidly: Evidence From 95 LDCs, 1976-85', *Economic Development and Cultural Change* 40: 523-44, April.

Dollar, D. amd A. Kraay (2000), 'Growth *is* Good for the Poor', mimeo, World Bank, Washington, D.C., March. (Background paper for the Bank's *World Development Report 2000/2001*.)

Duncan, R., S. Cuthbertson and M. Bosworth (1999), *Pursuing Economic Reform in the Pacific*, Pacific Studies Series No. 18, Asian Development Bank, Manila.

Duncan, R., S. Chand, Graham, B., T. Lawson and R.G. Duncan, *Exchange Rate Policy in Papua New Guinea*, Institute of National Affairs, Port Moresby.

Duncan, R. and T. Lawson, (1997), *Cost Structures in Papua New Guinea*, Institute of National Affairs, Port Moresby.

Economic Insights (1999), *Review of the MSG Trade Agreement*, Report for the South Pacific Forum Secretariat, Suva.

Edwards, S. (1993), 'Openness, Trade Liberalization, and Growth in Developing Countries', *Journal of Economic Literature* 31(3): 1358-93, September.

ESCAP (2000), *Non-Tariff Measures with Potentially Restrictive Market Access Implications Emerging in a Post-Uruguay Round Context*, Studies in Trade and Investment 40, Economic and Social Commission for Asia and the Pacific, United Nations, New York.

Fallon, J., T. King and J. Zeitsch, (1995), *Exchange rate Policy in Papua New Guinea*, Discussion Paper No. 64, Institute of National Affairs, Port Moresby.

FAO (1997), *SOFA'96*, Food and Agriculture Organisation, Rome (diskette of time series data).

Findlay, R. and S. Wellisz (eds.) (1993), *Five Small Open Economies*, Oxford University Press, London.

Fleming, E. and B. Hardaker (eds.) (1997) *Strategic Issues in the Economic Development of Melanesian Agriculture*, Development Issues No. 5, National Centre for Development Studies, ANU, Canberra.

Foroutan, F. (1998), *Does Membership in a Regional Preferential Trade Arrangement Make a Country More or Less Protectionist?*, Policy Research Working Paper 1898, Washington, D.C., World Bank.

Frankel, J.A. and Romer, D. (1999), 'Does Trade Cause Growth?', *American Economic Review*, 89(3): 379-99.

Gibson, J. (1997), *The Economics of Food Import Substitution in Papua New Guinea*, in E. Fleming and B. Hardaker (eds), *Strategic Issues in the Economic Development of Melanesian Agriculture*, Ch. 1, National Centre for Development Studies, Australian National University, Canberra.

— (1993), 'Import Substitution, Risk and Consumer Costs: the Papua New Guinea Sugar Industry', in J. Millet (ed), *Employment. Agriculture and Industrialisation*, Institute of National Affairs, Port Moresby.

Goode, W. (1998), *Dictionary of Trade Policy Terms*, Centre for International Economic Studies, Adelaide (revised edition).

Grilli, E.R. and M.C.Yang (1988), 'Primary Commodity Prices, Manufactured Goods Prices, and the Terms of Trade of Developing Countries: What the Long Run Shows', *World Bank Economic Review* 2(1): 1-48, January.

Grynberg, R. (1998), 'Fisheries Subsidies, the World Trade Organization, and the Pacific Island Tuna Industries', mimeo, National Centre for Development Studies, ANU, Canberra.

IMF (2000), *Small States: Meeting Challenges in the Global Economy*, Report of the Commonwealth Secretariat/World Bank Joint Task Force on Small States, Development Committee, March, Washington D.C.

INA (1999), *Factors Contributing to the Lack of Investment in Papua New Guinea: A Private Sector Survey*, Discussion Paper No.74, Institute of National Affairs, Port Moresby, July.

Jarrett, F.G. and K. Anderson (1989), *Growth, Structural Change and Economic Policy in Papua New Guinea: Implications for Agriculture*, Asia Pacific Press, ANU, Canberra.

Krugman, P. (1999), 'The Role of Geography in Development', in *Annual World Bank Conference in Development Economics 1998*, edited by J. Stiglitz and B. Pleskovic, The World Bank, Washington, D.C.

Levantis, T. (2000), *Papua New Guinea: Employment, Wages and Economic Development*, Asia Pacific School of Economics, Australian National University, and Management and Institute of National Affairs, Canberra and Port Moresby.

—(1997), *The Labour Market of Papua New Guinea; a study of its structure and policy implications*, PhD Thesis, Australian National University, Canberra.

Martin, W. and D. Mitra (1998), 'Productivity Growth and Convergence in Agriculture and Manufacturing', mimeo, Development Research Group, the World Bank, Washington, D.C., June.

Maskus, K. (2000), *Intellectual Property Rights in the Global Economy*, Institute for International Economics, Washington, D.C.

Mavroidis, P.C., H. Nordstrom and H. Horn (1999), 'Is the Use of the WTO Dispute Settlement System Biased?' Discussion Paper No. 2340, Centre for Economic Policy Research, London, December.

Michalopoulos, C. (1998), 'The Participation of Developing Countries in the WTO', Policy Research Working Paper 1906, World Bank, Washington, D.C., March.

PECC (1999), *Assessing APEC Individual Action Plans and their Contribution to APEC's Goals*, Trade Policy Forum, Pacific

Economic   Cooperation   Council,   available   at
http://www.fortunecity.com/business/turn/207/a

Petersmann, E-U. (1991), *Constitutional Functions and Constitutional Problems of International Economic Law*, Fribourg University Press, Fribourg.

Porter, M.E. (1990), *The Competitive Advantage of Nations*, The Free Press, New York.

Rapapatirana, S. (1997), *Trade Policies in Latin America and the Caribbean: Priorities, Progress and Prospects*, International Centre for Economic Growth, San Francisco.

REPIM Ltd. (1996), *Tariff Reform in an Expanded Indirect Taxation Structure*, report for the PNG Government and World Bank, Volume 1, May.

Roessler, F. (1985), 'The Scope, Limits and Function of the GATT Legal System', *The World Economy* 8(3): 287-98.

Rufina, P. (1997), *Food Import Substitution in Papua New Guinea: a case study of sugar production*, in E. Fleming and B. Hardaker (eds), *Strategic Issues in the Economic Development of Melanesian Agriculture*, Ch. 4, National Centre for Development Studies, Australian National University, Canberra.

Sachs, J.D. and A.M. Warner (1996), *Sources of Slow Growth in African Economies*, Harvard Institute of International Development, Cambridge MA.

— (1995), 'Economic Reform and the Process of Global Integration', *Brookings Papers on Economic Activity* 1: 1-95.

Scollay, R. (1998), *Free Trade Among Forum Island Countries*, report prepared for AusAid and the Government of New Zealand, South Pacific Forum Secretariat, Suva.

Snape, R.H., J. Adams and D. Morgan (1993), *Regional Trade Agreements; Implications and Options for Australia*, Department of Foreign Affairs and Trade, Canberra.

Stoeckel, A. and Corbet, H. (eds.) (1999), *Reason Verses Emotion: Requirements for a Successful WTO Round*, Rural Industries Research and Development Corporation, Canberra.

Stoeckel, A., K.K. Tang and W. McKibbin (1999), 'The Gains from Trade Liberalisation with Endogenous Productivity and Risk Premium Effects', Technical Paper for seminar on Reason Verses Emotion: Requirements for a Successful WTO Round, Sheraton Hotel, Seattle, December.

Temu, I. (1997), *Agriculture, Forestry and Fisheries*, in Temu (ed), *Papua New Guinea: A 20/20 Vision*, National Centre for Development Studies, Australian National University, Canberra.

Togolo, M. (1998), 'Report of the Consultative Implementation and Monitoring Council Proposals', National Economic Development Forum, 12-13 October, Port Moresby, unpublished.

Threadgold, M. (1988), *Bountious Bestowal: The Economic History of Norfolk Island*, Asia Pacific Press, ANU, Canberra.

Tyers, R. and K. Anderson (1992), *Disarray in World Food Markets: A Quantitative Assessment*, Cambridge University Press, Cambridge.

UNDP (2000), *Human Development Report 2000*, Oxford University Press, New York.

USITC (1997), *The Dynamic Effects of Trade Liberalization: An Empirical Analysis*. Publication 3069, US International Trade Commission, Washington, D.C., October.

Warr, P.G. (1994), 'Comparative and Competitive Advantage', *Asian-Pacific Economic Literature* 8(2): 1-14, November.

Winters, L.A. (2000), 'Trade Policy as Development Policy: Building on Fifty Years' Experience', Paper presented at UNCTAD X's High-level Round Table on Trade and Development, Bangkok, 12 February.

Woldekidan, B, (1994), *Short-Term Economic Consequences of Devaluing the Kina: A General Equilibrium Analysis for Papua New Guinea*, Special Publication No. 13, National Research Institute, Port Moresby.

Wonnacott, P. and M. Lutz (1989), 'Is there a Case for Free Trade Areas?', Chapter 2 of J.J. Schott (ed.), *Free Trade Areas and US Trade Policy*, Institute for International Economics, Washington, D.C.

World Bank (2000a), *World Development Indicators 1999* (CD-ROM), The World Bank, Washington, D.C.

— (2000b), *World Development Report 2000/2001: Attacking Poverty*, Oxford University Press, New York.

— (1997), *World Development Indicators 1997* (CD-ROM), The World Bank, Washington, D.C.

— (1996), *Papua New Guinea: Accelerating Agricultural Growth – An Action Plan*, Agricultural Operations Division, East Asia and Pacific Region, Washington, D.C.

WTO (1999), *Trade Policy Review of Papua New Guinea*, WTO Secretariat, Geneva.

— (1998a), Annual Report 1998, *Special topic: Globalization and Trade*, WTO Secretariat, Geneva.

— (1998b), *Trade Policy Review of the Solomon Islands*, WTO Secretariat, Geneva.

— (1998c), *Trade Policy Review of Trinidad and Tobago*, WTO Secretariat, Geneva.

— (1997), *Trade Policy Review of Fiji*, WTO Secretariat, Geneva.

www.ingramcontent.com/pod-product-compliance
Lightning Source LLC
Chambersburg PA
CBHW081240220326
41597CB00023BA/4222